EBURY PRESS AND BLUE SALT
BEHIND BARS IN BYCULLA

Jigna Vora is a crime reporter who has worked at the *Free Press Journal*, *Mid-day*, *Mumbai Mirror* and the *Asian Age*. She also practises healing, tarot card reading and astrology. She is currently researching for and writing web series and movies.

Behind Bars in Byculla

━

My Days *in* Prison

JIGNA VORA

BLUE SALT

EBURY
PRESS

An imprint of Penguin Random House

EBURY PRESS

USA | Canada | UK | Ireland | Australia
New Zealand | India | South Africa | China | Singapore

Ebury Press is part of the Penguin Random House group of companies
whose addresses can be found at global.penguinrandomhouse.com

Published by Penguin Random House India Pvt. Ltd
4th Floor, Capital Tower 1, MG Road,
Gurugram 122 002, Haryana, India

Penguin
Random House
India

First published in Ebury Press and Blue Salt by Penguin Random House India 2019

ISBN 9780143446910

Typeset in Adobe Caslon Pro by Manipal Digital Systems, Manipal

Printed at Repro India Limited

For my loving son, and my guru Satish Kaku

CONTENTS

Prologue   ix

1. Entering Laal Gate   1
2. Barrack No. 2   10
3. Spider Woman   17
4. The Saffron Lady   26
5. First Encounter with the Police   39
6. Ruler of the Jail   48
7. Joining *Mumbai Mirror*   59
8. Usha Maa   70
9. Meeting a Stalwart: Jyotirmoy Dey   76
10. The Outsiders   83
11. The Rise and Fall   94
12. Jail's Mandakini   103

CONTENTS

13. Collateral Damage   112
14. The Killing of J. Dey   121
15. Dog Eat Dog   128
16. Days of Destruction   138
17. Caste Factor   153
18. Unlikely Saviour   157
19. Cheerleaders   160
20. The Birthday Gift   172
21. Cheats   192
22. My World War III   201
23. Return of Rajan   212
24. The Trial   217
25. Accused No. 11 Acquitted   231

Epilogue: The Mystery   241
Acknowledgements   247

PROLOGUE

Friday, 11 May 2018

A resounding gunshot echoed through the corridors of Himanshu Roy's home at Suniti Apartments, Nariman Point, Mumbai. His wife and two domestic helpers rushed inside his room. A pool of blood streamed around the fallen body of Himanshu Roy, an officer of the coveted Indian Police Service from the batch of 1988. Moments before, he had placed the cold barrel of his licensed revolver in his mouth and pulled the trigger. The bullet had entered through his mouth and pierced through his skull. Roy's driver, a constable with the Mumbai Police, informed the Control Room about the incident. Authorities were quick to respond. Sirens from ambulances and police jeeps converged towards Gen. J. Bhosale Road, where Suniti Apartments stood tall against the Mumbai skyline. Roy was rushed to Bombay Hospital. Doctors hurried to check on him, but the wounds were the work of a man trained in the use of firearms. He had left nothing to chance. Additional Director General of Police (Establishment) Himanshu Roy, aged fifty-four, was declared dead at 1.47 p.m. His body was taken to GT Hospital at Crawford Market for a post-mortem under tight security. The hospital was metres away from the police commissioner's office, the premises of which had also housed top officers of Mumbai Police, including Himanshu Roy. Tributes from fellow cops, politicians, top-notch lawyers and media personnel began pouring in. The news flashed over TV channels and flooded social media timelines. An entire city mourned the death of a super cop.

Roy had been fighting a prolonged battle with renal cancer. He had been operated upon in the year 2000, but the cancer had returned with a vengeance nearly sixteen years later and spread to his brain and his bones. This had rendered him out of action for the past two years. His skin had darkened due to chemotherapy. He had been reduced to a pale shadow of the imposing personality that had once made criminals cower with fear. The bulky muscles that often bulged in his shirts during press conferences and flexed on to the front pages of newspapers had grown frail and weak. He had lost a lot of weight. A white beard had covered his jawline.

But even in the depression of battling a fatal disease, the super cop gave no warning that he had made up his mind. Or maybe he did. The evening before his death, he took out time for what he was most obsessed about: a hard workout at the gym. He was a devout follower of Lord Hanuman, the god of strength. A photograph of Bajrangbali standing in all his glory had once adorned the wall of Himanshu's office at the Crime Branch. He would visit the Hanuman temple near his office every Saturday. And on the day he killed himself, he had eaten a good breakfast for the first time in several days. The man who loved eating tandoori chicken asked his cook to prepare his favourite dish for lunch. These could have been signs that he intended to continue his fight with the enemy that had plagued his body.

Or maybe he wanted to relive some semblance of his best days before breathing his last.

Perhaps it was the latter, because he later walked into his bedroom and wrote the suicide note that was eventually found in a folder by investigators. The note read that he was committing suicide due to the 'frustration' of his illness. Investigators also believed that he had taken out his revolver from his locker a day earlier. His note said, 'No one is responsible for my suicide.'

As joint commissioner of police (Crime), Himanshu Roy had handled extremely sensational cases like the Laila Khan murder, the Kohinoor Mill rape, and a multi-crore diamond heist in Goregaon. He had also led the investigation in the high-profile Indian Premier League betting scandal. But the murder of crime journalist

J. Dey in 2011 had put him in the media spotlight like no other case. It was covered extensively in the media because one of their own had been murdered in cold blood. The shootout was carried out by the hitmen of underworld don Chhota Rajan. Ten men were arrested, and Rajan was also charge-sheeted in the case. But in a bizarre twist to the entire episode, thirty-seven-year-old Jigna Vora, a female journalist who was then deputy bureau chief of the *Asian Age*, was taken into police custody for instigating the murder.

That journalist was I.

'We have thirty-six damning transcripts of Jigna Vora and Chhota Rajan plotting the murder of J. Dey,' Roy had told a delegation of journalists who went to meet him in the presence of then home minister R.R. Patil.

The case was heard over a period of nearly seven years. Lives were destroyed, and families torn apart. My promising career was shattered to pieces, and could never be put together again. On 2 May 2018, the Maharashtra Control of Organized Crime Act (MCOCA) court convicted Chhota Rajan and eight other accused in the case. But I was acquitted after seven long years, a part of which I spent in prison.

This is my story.

1

ENTERING LAAL GATE

9 December 2011

I stripped down to the last piece of cloth on my body. Two lady constables flanked me inside a dingy room in the Byculla Jail. The room had no windows. But the lack of ventilation did not suffocate me as much as the humiliation did. The crassness with which the constables made me shed my clothes shook me to the core. For the two women, barely in their thirties, it was routine. For me, even the dim orange glare from the tiny bulb felt like a violation.

'Take off your underwear,' the stout constable said.

'Please,' I said with folded hands. 'I am menstruating.'

'Doesn't matter,' she said. 'Make it quick!'

I pulled my underwear down to my ankles and stepped out of it. The constable checked my undergarments for contraband. To my utter disbelief, she even checked the sanitary pad I had worn without batting an eyelid.

'Now,' the stout constable said, 'sit down and stand up. Five times.'

As a law graduate and a journalist, squatting, I knew, was a police drill, to check contraband that one may be carrying in their private parts. My body shivered, as I did what I was asked to. I squatted, five times, my vagina exposed, blood dripping down my thighs. Once sure, they asked me to dress up and step out of the room. I cleaned up and put my clothes back on. I picked up the plastic bag in which I had carried a comb, toothpaste, toothbrush and a bar of Lux soap that my lawyer Jayesh Vithlani had handed me when the cops dragged me out of the courtroom to be taken to the jail.

When I stepped outside the dingy room, I was ordered to wait in the reception area. The heightened ceiling had two fans rotating slowly, their blades covered with thick dust. Even though it was December and the weather bearable, I felt the sweat roll down my ribs. Two male constables with self-loading rifles stared at me, from top to bottom. They exchanged a look that conveyed a voyeuristic pleasure of knowing what I had just been through. Something rose inside my throat, a scream perhaps; but whatever it was, I held it in and gazed at the dirty floor. When I looked up again, the constables were still staring.

I covered myself with the woollen shawl that I had purchased from Sikkim, where I had spent a blissful vacation only a few months ago.

A woman constable then led to me towards Laal Gate. True to its name, it was a huge iron gate painted in red. To me, it carried a sense of foreboding that once I crossed this gate, my life of freedom would be dictated by the rules of the jail.

As a reporter, I had filed stories of various accused, such as Sujata Nikhalje, the wife of Chhota Rajan; Fahmeeda, a bomb blast accused; Maria Susairaj, an accused in the sensational Neeraj Grover murder case; Jaya Chheda, accused of murdering her husband. I had never thought that I would one day be following in the footsteps of these women. Crossing that threshold changed my life for ever—in ways that could never be undone. All the identities I had worked so hard to build—a dutiful daughter to my parents, a loving mother to my son, a woman journalist who fought to carve her space in the male-dominated bastion of crime reporting—were reduced to a four-digit number in the annals of that government prison. The undertrial number that jail officials assigned to me was 1193. I was ordered to sit under a huge tree near the entrance. I rested my head against the thick trunk as the constable completed her paperwork.

I had lived life on my own terms. I have never been concerned about others' opinion about me. But as I sat there, one thought spun through my mind constantly: *What will people think of me?*

Soon, I was taken to the jailer's office. Aagya madam, as the jailer was known, sat in her chair, while a woman,

3

wearing a nightie, wailed beside her. The jailer gave me a stern look as I passed through her room, which led to the barracks. I was put in Circle Number 1. Due to logistics and security reasons, the various complexes in a jail are called circles. There were six barracks in Circle 1 and two barracks in Circle 2. Byculla Jail comprised two circles for women.

Depending upon your crime, and later, your behaviour (if someone creates nuisance or does not follow rules), inmates are shifted from Circle 1 to Circle 2.

The lady constables knew about my impending arrival. It was probably due to the constant media coverage that my case had received. The inmates too seemed to know who I was. I walked past a group of inmates, who sat in a semicircle. My arrival deviated their attention.

'Look,' said one of them and elbowed the other. 'The new whore has arrived.'

The barrack was like a dormitory, with stained walls and black limestone flooring. The constables gave me a thin sleeping mat, an aluminium plate and a mug. In that large room full of women and children, I was left to find my own space. A plaque on the wall told me that the barrack had been built only nine years ago. With very little ventilation and a filthy stench, it was dirtier than a warehouse. There were nearly forty women in that room. Some looked comfortable, singing songs and chit-chatting, or bonding by picking lice from another's head, while others just kept to themselves. There were infants howling and children playing around the room. 'Why are there kids here?' I asked the room, but no one bothered to answer me. I put down my head on my knees and sat there, hoping it would all disappear when I looked up again. When I did, I found a boy, barely five years old, staring at me.

'Aunty, why are you crying?'

I sniffed.

'Don't worry, God will make everything right,' he said and ran off.

I thought about my son. He is twelve years old. How would he react to all this? What would he think of me? Would he believe that I had done something wrong? The thoughts made me numb.

The undertrial inmates had their own way of allocating space to the other inmates, depending on their reputation. Those at the lower rung of the barrack's social ladder received barely enough space to sleep. Relative luxury was accorded to those who were higher in the hierarchy of power. One of the women had pointed me towards a corner. 'That is your area,' she said. 'Stay within your limit.'

At 5.30 p.m., dinner was served inside the barracks. On my aluminium plate, I had two chapattis, dal and some vegetables. Strands of black hair floated in the watery dal. I put the plate aside and wept again. Pangs of pain cramped my stomach. I had hardly eaten since my arrest. I felt weak and exhausted, but I could not bring myself to eat the food I had been served. An African undertrial, who had been observing me from a distance, sensed my predicament.

'You are the journalist, aren't you?' she said.

I nodded.

'Did you commit the murder?'

'No,' I said, as if it meant anything. 'No,' I emphasized.

'I know,' she said. 'You're a good person.'

I didn't know how to respond.

'Are you hungry?' she asked.

I shook my head. She stared at me, reached inside her pockets and pulled out a coarse piece of bread.

'Eat,' she said. 'Eat it.'

I took the piece of bread from her hands. Soon she sensed a prison guard approaching and rushed back to her place. Her kindness felt nice. But I just did not have the appetite.

The barracks were locked down at 6 p.m., a procedure that was known as *bandi*. Huge, black, iron locks were put on all doors at that time. Doors too were made of iron rods, which allowed inmates to speak to those on the other side.

As I wiped the tears off my cheeks, a woman in her thirties, sitting diagonally opposite, watched me intently. She wore a blue track pant and white T-shirt. Her hair was tied in a neat bun, clasped with a black hair clip. A thick, red tilak ran through the middle of her forehead. Pictures of Hindu gods and goddesses were hung from the iron rods behind her. The most prominent one was that of Goddess Kali, the destroyer of evil. The woman occupied three times the space that the other inmates had. She summoned me to her temple-like corner and introduced herself as Paromita Chakraborty.

'Aren't you Jigna Vora?' she asked, in fluent English.

I shivered at the baritone of her voice and replied hesitantly, 'Y-Y-Yes.'

Paromita stared right into my eyes, measuring me perhaps. 'Don't worry. You'll be fine.'

I heaved a sigh of relief. She turned around and pulled out an open packet of potato wafers.

'Eat,' she said.

I hesitated, but the intensity of her glare made me pick up one wafer and put it in my mouth. The wafer crunched loudly under my teeth.

'Tea?' she asked.

'No,' I said.

'Okay,' she said. 'Go back to your place.'

I did what I was told. At around 8.30 p.m., the inmates prepared to sleep, as the television in the barrack wasn't working. They bundled their extra clothes into their dupattas to use as a pillow, and I copied them. I could hear the chatter, most of them discussing their court hearings. I thought about my son and wept.

Another inmate slept next to me, close enough that if I didn't turn over very carefully in my sleep, I might land on top of her. She smelt much like the mouldy barrack. I wondered if I would stink the same way if I had to spend more days here. I yearned to relieve myself, but I resisted, not wanting to witness the sight of a dirty toilet. I stood up and paced along the little space by the walls. An inmate pulled her blanket off her face.

'Go sleep, whore,' she said. 'Why are you disturbing all of us?'

I raised my little finger, indicating that I needed to use the bathroom. The inmate contorted her face in irritation and pointed towards the toilet.

Finally giving up, I walked through the narrow passage, past blue drums that stored water for daily use. Four Indian-style toilets, each of them equally dirty and stained, awaited me. I held my breath and entered through a door that only covered my torso once I planted my soles on the footrest. My head and the other end of my body were completely exposed. I prayed for some privacy.

I returned to my place and lay down at my designated space. The lights, I learnt, were never turned off. As a rule, they are switched on, twenty-four hours a day, seven days a week. As I lay there under the lights, I knew what having my own space meant. To own a single bed in a small flat in suburban Mumbai. I remembered the tantrums I would throw if my grandmother would accidentally switch on the light while I was sleeping. Here, I couldn't do a thing about it. With the hard floor under my back, I spent most of the night staring at the ceiling and thinking about my son.

I had just fallen asleep when a sudden commotion woke me up. It was 5.30 a.m., time to wake up so that the jail officials could do a headcount. Each inmate was paired with another accused of a similar crime and asked to sit in the centre of the barrack. The gravity of the crime decided the order. Accused chain snatchers, pickpockets, robbers and murderers—all sat in order. I sat alone. I was the only one booked under the stringent Maharashtra Control of Organized Crime Act (MCOCA) that the government had formed to combat organized crime and terrorism. I looked down as the inmates stared and chattered.

'Is she a terrorist? Is she from the underworld?'

2

BARRACK NO. 2

Everyone wanted to know Jigna Vora. In that pity-worthy barrack, I had achieved sudden fame. The women were curious about me, each one of them asking blatant questions one after another. 'Are you a member of the Chhota Rajan gang?' 'You work for the underworld, no?' 'Did you commit the murder?'

I ignored all their questions. They were more like accusations. Most of them talked to me and looked at me with the certainty that I was a murderer. Some were unsure if I had committed the crime. But I stuck to my lawyer's advice that I should not indulge in unnecessary conversations. He had warned me that cops and crooks both have informers inside the jail.

Barrack No. 2 in Circle 1, where I was placed, was reserved for old women, or those with kids or severe medical conditions. After the morning headcount, I wondered if I would be able to take a bath. I asked a thin woman in her fifties, Samaira Bibi, who had slept next to me, about the bathing area. She pointed to the same dingy toilet I had used the previous night.

'Can I get some hot water?' I asked.

'Half a bucket of warm water is allowed for the kids,' she said. 'Adults don't get it easily.'

Another inmate told me that a bucket of hot water was reserved only for the big sharks.

I queued up outside the toilet, waiting for my turn. Other inmates tied their dupattas above the doors of the toilets to cover the upper half of their bodies. In that reeking toilet, I followed the other inmates and knotted my dupatta over the two rusty nails on the walls before bathing.

After bathing, some of the inmates settled down to read the newspaper. Marathi newspapers were provided in all the barracks. Most inmates had read about my case over the past ten days. They continued to prod me in the hope of learning more details. Suddenly, from amidst the chaos around me, Paromita Chakraborty, the tilak-wearing woman who had offered me chips, pulled me away. It seemed like she was trying to protect me.

I couldn't help but ask her, 'Why is everybody so eager to speak with me?'

'You're all over the papers,' Paromita said.

'So?'

'They think you're influential. Being close to a powerful inmate like you can earn them some leniency from the cops.'

11

We were interrupted by the call for breakfast. One of the inmates, Usha Maa, was the warden of the barracks and wore a yellow sari as a mark of identification. She was serving a life sentence for scheming with her lover to murder her husband. She was in charge of distributing food to the inmates and acted as an intermediary between the undertrial inmates and the cops. Everyone queued up for breakfast. The food was distributed with strict rationing. I was about to line up too, but Paromita stopped me. Tania, a young Bangladeshi undertrial who did odd jobs for Paromita, got a plateful of the poha and a mug of tea for her, and me. I picked the rice flakes with my hands, but they were coarse and dry. The tea was thin, more water than milk. Tasteless, but I somehow managed to gulp it down without throwing up. I saw a lot of food being wasted.

'Who cooks here?' I asked Paromita.

'The men cook the food,' she said. 'Women are not allowed inside the kitchen. The jail authorities say women steal a lot of food items for personal consumption.'

A young girl, about two years of age, playfully tugged at my rust-coloured kurta. I ruffled her curly hair. Her mother came around and introduced herself as Nazia. She had been accused in a kidnapping case and had been in jail for the past four months. I also learnt that Samaira Bibi had been jailed for abetting her daughter-in-law's suicide. Her husband and son had also been imprisoned at the Arthur Road Jail in the same case, but her husband had died of medical complications in the prison itself. The authorities informed Samaira Bibi only three days after the death had occurred, by dragging her to the morgue. She appeared to be a religious woman who always had a prayer on her lips.

Paromita asked if I was aware that Chhota Rajan's wife Sujata Nikhalje had also been lodged in the same jail. I didn't know what to say. As a reporter, I had worked on many stories about Sujata's arrest in an extortion case. She had led a hunger strike inside the jail to highlight the bad conditions. I had written a story about the strike too. It felt strange, a twist of fate, that long after Sujata had been released, I had landed up in the same jail.

Lunch was served early at 10.30 a.m., brought in the same huge aluminium containers. Tania brought me a plate filled with rotis, rice, dal and brinjal curry. I picked a roti between my fingers, and it was at least five times thicker than the thin chapatis I was used to eating from my Gujarati grandmother's kitchen. I could see worms inside the brinjal, and so I only ate a few morsels of rice. Later, I washed my plate in the toilet and was on the way back to my barrack when a woman in her twenties, holding an infant in her arms, called out to me. Her baby boy's stomach was bloated and the boy would just not stop crying.

'Didi?' she asked. 'Did you eat?'

'Yes,' I replied.

'Do you need anything else?'

'No.'

'Let me know if I can help in any way,' she said.

13

I nodded and walked away. Samaira Bibi told me that the woman's name was Sangeeta. She was a ragpicker and had been jailed for some petty crime.

'Don't speak to that woman,' Samaira Bibi said.

'Why?'

'She is sick. Diseased.'

'What happened to her?'

Samaira Bibi spoke after a long pause, uttering the word with much caution: 'AIDS.'

I felt sorry for Sangeeta. Other inmates would not even talk to her for the fear of contracting the virus. Even though I was away from Sangeeta, I could still hear her baby crying.

There was a bandi in the barracks from 12 noon to 3 p.m. Some inmates slept, while some watched Doordarshan on the small television that was mounted on the wall. Inmates discussed their love for serials like *Ramayan* and *Mahabharat*. The mothers breastfed their infants. The inmates stuck to their groups. Pickpockets had their own group, same as the robbers.

Much like life outside, social divisions inside Byculla Jail arose out of occupation. On the boards outside, the jail declared itself as a 'rehabilitation centre', but each group was holed up in a corner, recruiting more personnel in their gangs and marking their territories for future operations. More than rehabilitation, the centre seemed to offer an opportunity for the criminals to grow their existing groups.

Around 1.30 p.m., a lady constable called out my name.

'Someone is here to meet you,' she said. 'In the *mulaqaat* room.'

'How do I go there?'

'Follow me,' she said.

I stood up hurriedly and followed her to the judicial area. I wondered who my visitor would be and I hoped that he or she had come with some good news.

On the way, the jailer, Pushpa Kadam, happened to notice me and cast a long look at my attire.

'Stop!' she said.

I froze.

She turned to the constable. 'Why is Jigna not wearing a dupatta?'

'Sorry, madam,' the constable said.

'Ensure it never happens again,' Pushpa said before walking away.

The constable chided me for not knowing the rules I had never been told about. A dupatta was compulsory for every inmate leaving the barracks. She warned that I would not be allowed to meet my visitors if I did not wear a dupatta. I promised to keep it handy in the future. Then, she let me into the mulaqaat room where I was surprised to find my estranged father waiting for me. The scent of alcohol was evident on his breath.

'Why are you here?' I asked.

'To meet you,' he said. 'I was worried.'

'You found the time to meet me after two weeks?'

'Well,' he said. 'You won't be getting out anytime soon.'

'What?' I shouted. 'What are you saying?'

'No, no,' he said. 'I meant, I have no money really.'

'So, what do you want me to do?'

'Give me some money. I can come to visit you every day.' He paused. 'You are my daughter. You'll give me the money, right?'

I choked as if a stone had been forced down my throat. 'I don't have any money.'

I could not stand the sight of his face for a minute longer. I stormed out of the room and rushed back to my barrack. My father's alcoholism had destroyed my childhood and my family. The man who once drove a Mercedes Benz in Dubai had never cared to save a dime for his family. His lifestyle and alcohol had taken all his glory away. And at a time when I needed a few words of comfort, there he was, unashamedly asking for money. I shuddered with anger. Tears rolled down my eyes as I sat in the corner of the barrack. My father had always cared about his bottle, but never his daughter.

16

3

SPIDER WOMAN

One morning, there was a huge commotion. A dark, short woman, clad in white shorts and a T-shirt, had climbed up several feet along the walls of the barracks with the help of the pipes. A lack of judgement or a slight slip in balance would mean she would fall to her death. But it seemed like Sapna Pereira had the dexterity of a trapeze artist. She continued to scale higher while we craned our necks to see what exactly she was up to. A repeat offender at the Byculla Jail, Sapna was a pickpocket from Mumbai's Juhu area. Her climbing stunts too were not new. This is why some of the old-timers in the barracks turned a blind eye towards Sapna's antics. Some of the concerned inmates rushed to alert the warden Usha Maa and other jail authorities.

'Sapna!' she called out. 'Come down!'

'No!' Sapna shouted from atop. 'No way!'

'Why?' Usha Maa said. 'Why are you doing this?'

'Because these *behenchod* cops don't take me to court.'

Sapna had been angry with the policemen. On several occasions when her case could have come up for hearing, the cops did not take her along. The court dates were a chance to step out of the stuffy barracks and breathe some fresh air. Each one of us in the jail awaited them. But the cops from the local arms unit of the Mumbai Police who were entrusted with the responsibility of accompanying the inmates from jail to court and back were least bothered. Working in the local arms unit was nothing but a punishment posting for these police officials. Seething in their own frustration, the cops were least interested in coordinating with jail authorities for court dates. This left many like Sapna angered. But her way of venting was different from others.

'Sapna,' Usha Maa shouted again. 'You'll hurt yourself. Please come down.'

'These police-wallahs never show up for my court visit,' Sapna said. 'They do it on purpose.'

'No, Sapna. It is not like that!'

'These fuckers don't want me to get bail!' Sapna screamed. 'They want me to rot in here for ever!'

She climbed higher and reached a ledge and balanced herself. There was just enough space for one person to stand, but she seemed at home. And then, the unimaginable happened. She slid her shorts down her legs, and took off her T-shirt. She stood up there, completely naked. More cops arrived on the scene, including Constable Waseema

Shaikh, who had been a part of the strip search conducted on me. The cops were angry, but they kept pleading with Sapna to climb down. Sapna hurled abuses at them. Only when the cops assured her that they would take all steps to ensure her next court visit would not be missed, Sapna decided that it was time for her to give up. She came down the pipes, as easily as she had made her way up. The reconciliatory tone of the cops vanished as soon as she landed on the ground, but they did not take any further action because it was close to noon, and about time for the bandi. The flushing red look on the faces of the cops conveyed that, soon enough, they would teach Sapna a lesson she would not forget.

That afternoon, Sapna came up to me in the barracks and introduced herself. She was still wearing the same white shorts and T-shirt. I noticed that she had very short hair and a flat nose. As we sat with our backs against the walls, she spoke in typical Mumbaiya slang.

'Oye, item, don't worry,' she said. 'You will get out of jail soon.'

I nodded. A constable was standing at a distance, and she happened to look our way. The cops always kept a tab on what went on inside the barracks. It was essential to controlling the place.

'Never fear these motherfuckers,' Sapna said and pointed her eyes in the constable's direction. 'They can't do nothing to us.'

I nodded again.

'Look at me,' she said. 'I've been in and out of this jail for the last ten years.'

'Really?'

'Yes,' she said. 'How is your son?'

'My family is taking care of him.'

'I have a daughter too,' she said. 'People call me a thief. But the poor girl has lost her vision. I need the money to get her operated.'

I felt sorry for the woman, but I was in a grave situation myself. 'What about your bail?'

'I don't have money for that either,' she said. 'And these *gaandu*s don't take me to the court for my hearings. They've detained me for the last six months. How am I supposed to get out?'

'I understand.'

'I hope Jaya Maa comes back soon,' Sapna said. 'She has promised to help me with the bail bond.'

Then, she abruptly stood up and left. I noticed she never referred to the cops without adding an expletive, and she had extreme contempt for any form of authority.

Sapna and her antics were not news to me. As a journalist, I had read stories about her. The woman had once worked in the office of a politician in Mumbai. Her husband, Issac, a native of Karnataka, had died in a road accident. Sapna was left alone to take care of her teenage daughter who was visually challenged. She claimed to have taken her daughter to a hospital in New Delhi more than forty times, but the doctors suggested that she could probably be cured only in the United States. Sapna soon began saving money to make a trip to the US someday.

Once, Sapna had been to Mangaluru to check the status of an old robbery case. When she got back to her hotel room, she found cash worth Rs 47,000 and gold worth Rs 1.5 lakh missing from her luggage along with her and her daughter's passports. An angry Sapna did not know what to do. To grab attention, she climbed up on a mobile tower. The drama that went on for hours was widely reported by the media. While the police had recovered the cash and gold from the accused hotel staff, they could not find the passports as the accused had set them afire.

Paromita warned me against speaking with Sapna.

'Why?' I asked.

'She's a nuisance. The incident you witnessed in the morning happens all the time when she is here.'

'Is it?'

'Yes,' Paromita said. 'And she will ask you for money.'

I decided to keep my distance from Sapna. In the evening, the cops called Sapna outside the barracks on the pretext of some work, and took her to an isolated room. Inside Barrack No. 2, I heard her screams, and wished that the cops would stop beating her. After the cops had extracted their revenge for the trouble she had put them through, Sapna limped her way back to Barrack No. 5. Her face was swollen, and she was wailing like a child now. The beating seemed to have crushed her morale, but Paromita was sure that Sapna would be back to her ways sooner than anyone could imagine.

Over the next few days, Sapna made a lot of effort to draw me into conversation. But I stuck to my lawyer's advice and responded in as few words as possible. The inmates always judged each other, and they always had an opinion whether or not an undertrial had committed the crime she had been accused of. I learnt from Sapna that most inmates thought I had committed the crime. But I couldn't care less.

The constable, Waseema Shaikh, was unusually cordial with me thereafter. She also warned me that any form of friendship with Sapna would only land me in more trouble. The terror of Sapna Pereira was such that even judges were embarrassed by her antics and would make all attempts to ensure she did not land up in their courts. After what Waseema had put me through during the strip search, I was surprised that she was being so friendly with me.

Once Sapna excitedly walked up to me and began narrating an incident. On a late night in 2007, Sapna had worn a short red skirt, high boots and make-up. Then she had made her way to Juhu, which was her preferred area of operation. She had stood at the signal near Bollywood superstar Amitabh Bachchan's bungalow, and waved her thumb suggestively at passing cars, a sign that she needed to hitch a ride. Several luxury cars passed by, and then a white ambassador stopped. She rushed towards the car.

The tinted windows lowered, and a bald man in his fifties, sitting on the rear seat, popped his head out.

'Need a lift?' he asked.

She cast a flirtatious glance at the bald man. 'Yes.'

'Get inside,' the man said, grinning.

She ran to the other side and hopped into the car. The driver put the car into gear. As the car drove on, Sapna moved promiscuously close to the bald man. He put his hand on her thigh. She smiled. Encouraged, he moved his hand higher to her waist. She moved closer to him. The man leaned into her, put his hand on her breast and squeezed. Sapna screamed at the top of her lungs and the car screeched to a halt in the middle of the road.

'Bastard!' Sapna shouted. 'Are you trying to rape me?'

The man raised his hands in the air. 'No, no.'

Sapna raised her voice. 'Oh yes, you are! You saw a helpless woman on the road, and you tried to rape her!'

'Please,' the man said. 'Please don't raise your voice.'

Though it was late at night, there was a considerable crowd on the road as Juhu is usually crowded at that time. Sapna could see heads turn in the car's direction.

'I will scream now,' Sapna said. 'Your lecherous act will be all over the newspapers!'

'Don't do this.' The man clasped his hands tightly. 'I'll give you anything you want.'

'Hmm.' Sapna lowered her voice.

'What do you have in your wallet? Show me.'

23

'Three-and-a-half thousand.' The man pulled a brown wallet out of the back pocket of his trousers and opened it wide. 'Take it, take it.'

Sapna collected the money, and her gaze fell on the man's wrist. He promptly gave her the wristwatch too.

'Good,' Sapna said as she rolled the watch down her hands. She leaned into the man and ran her fingers over the chain he was wearing around his neck. 'Gold?'

'Yes, yes,' the man said.

He pulled the chain off and handed it over. Sapna collected the loot and stepped out of the car. The driver sped off like he had seen a ghost. Sapna laughed on her way back to the Juhu signal, waiting for another scapegoat to drive her way. About three months after that incident, the police arrested her in a pickpocketing case. She was produced at the Andheri Metropolitan Court and led into the courtroom. As her name was announced in the court, she looked up at the judge and realized it was the same bald man she had looted! The judge's face turned white when the reality dawned upon him. Sapna cast a knowing glance at the judge, a warning that she would reveal the incident in the court. Hurriedly, the judge signed her bail order and let her go!

Back in the jail, I laughed loud until my ribs hurt. Sapna insisted that she was a thief, and a blackmailer, but not a prostitute. She had also tried reforming her life, but in spite of all her attempts, she could not get a respectable job. She stole, but only to survive and save for her daughter's treatment. That was all she knew to do for a living.

In April 2012, Sapna was released on bail. Two years later, in 2014, when I was glancing through the newspapers, I read another article in the paper about her. She had climbed up an advertising hoarding in Byculla and caused complete chaos for four hours. It was only after police and fire brigade officials gave her the assurance that the government would help her with her daughter's eye operation that she came down. And then I thought about how she had climbed up the wall in the barracks in jail and created the ruckus.

4

THE SAFFRON LADY

On 28 September 2008, two bombs ripped apart a tiny locality in Malegaon, where a large part of the population was Muslim. The same day, another bomb exploded in Gujarat's Modasa town. More than half a dozen people were killed and hundreds severely injured, even as the investigators said that they were low-intensity bombs. The probe into the Malegaon blasts made a surprising and controversial revelation—involvement of the Hindu right wing. The term 'saffron terror' was coined, and used widely. For a country where terrorists were always Muslims, the accusation of Hindus being bombers was hard to swallow. Interestingly, at the helm of the investigation was Anti-Terrorist Squad (ATS) chief Hemant Karkare, a Hindu.[1]

---

[1] '10 Facts About the Malegaon Blasts', *Wire*, 25 June 2015, https://thewire.in/law/10-facts-about-the-malegaon-blasts

The story about Hindu right wing's involvement was first reported by the *Indian Express*. It was a big miss for crime reporters like me working in other papers. From the very next day, I began tracking the story, following as many leads as possible. The ATS had made several arrests in the case, and one of the accused was Pragya Singh Thakur, a *sadhvi* (lady monk).[2] The sadhvi added more spectacle to the already dramatic terror probe. The investigators had found that the explosive was fitted in a motorcycle bearing the licence number MH15 P4572, which they claimed belonged to the sadhvi.

Always clad in a saffron robe, Pragya, who was picked up from a village near Surat, had taken sanyas in the 2006 Kumbh Mela at Allahabad. In the early 1990s, she had been an active leader of the Akhil Bhartiya Vidyarthi Parishad (ABVP). In her college days, she was known to fearlessly ride motorcycles and beat up men who harassed women on the roads.

---

[2] Smruti Koppikar, 'A Myth Blasted?' in 'Terror Probe Malegaon', *Outlook*, 10 November 2008, pp. 30–31, https://books.google.co.in/books?id=PzEEAAAAMBAJ&pg=PA35&lpg=PA35&dq=ats +arrests+pragya+thakur+malegaon+blast+in+2008&source=bl& ots=qh8QM3IOwO&sig=ACfU3U0E9TH8jjRHPSVkdb7LL vj-1i4PWA&hl=en&sa=X&ved=2ahUKEwjXhP6Yve3hAhU Y2o8KHSG3BqU4RhDoATADegQICRAB#v=onepage&q= ats%20arrests%20pragya%20thakur%20malegaon%20blast%20 in%202008&f=false

As I followed the story, my interest in Pragya grew with every passing day, pushing me to prod my sources in the police and the ATS to tell more about her.

Fate brought me face to face with her at Byculla Jail.

Pragya was in the high-security cell, to the right of Barrack No. 2, where I was lodged. Hers was a solitary cell, with an attached toilet and bathroom. Her neighbour in the next solitary cell was Fahmeeda Ansari, who was facing death penalty in the 2003 case of twin bomb blasts at the Gateway of India and Zaveri Bazaar. Her case was pending for appeal in the high court, for which she had been shifted from Pune's Yerwada Jail to Mumbai.

Pragya was off limits to other inmates for her own protection. A woman police constable guarded her cell attentively round the clock. After the inmates were locked up in the barracks post-bandi, I would observe, through the gaps between the iron rods, the constable accompanying the sanyasin for a walk within the jail compound in the evening. I had noticed that Pragya was in pain and needed support while she took her evening strolls. It was rumoured that she had been subjected to severe torture by the ATS, which had led to the deterioration of her physical condition. At the same time, she was also a matter of national debate and political importance. The jail officials undoubtedly had to take utmost care that nothing untoward happened to her. For extra caution, no inmate could even utter a word to Pragya, unless she initiated the conversation. Though she was in solitary confinement, inmates could talk with her through the iron rods. Because of her solitary confinement, she was not allowed to come out during non-bandi hours or mingle with other inmates.

By the last week of December 2011, around Christmas, I had shifted from the corner of the barrack and closer to the door. The acute stuffiness of the corner had worsened my asthma. The door allowed some ventilation, and also gave me a clear view of the cell where Pragya was lodged. One morning, around 10 a.m., Pragya, who was standing outside her cell, happened to notice me. She smiled and gestured with her hands for me to come over. I went closer to her and for the first time met the woman in the saffron robe. Her hair was cropped to a length above her neck, and a red tilak lined her forehead. She spoke polished, scholarly Hindi.

'People told me you're here,' she said. 'I have been waiting to talk to you.'

'Me too.'

She pulled out the Hindi edition of the *Navbharat Times*, and pointed her finger to a headline. 'Have you read this?'

I shook my head. I had developed an intense phobia of the newspapers. As a journalist, I always took pride in seeing my name in the bylines of the stories I had broken. If a few days passed without my byline on exclusive stories, I would feel restless. But now, I feared seeing the newspapers with reports about my case. The mere mention of my name in articles would give me jitters. The media had already branded me as a criminal. Most of what was printed against me was malicious libel. The character assassination from people who were once my fellows made things worse for me.

They wrote about how I liked visiting spas or eating momos, as if that was a crime. They wrote about love affairs I never knew existed. They wrote about fortunes I never knew I owned.

Sadhvi Pragya told me that the article was about a witness recording a statement under Section 164 of the Cr.PC (Criminal Procedure Code) against me. Such a statement recorded in the presence of a magistrate holds weight even if the witness turns hostile at a later stage of the trial, unlike a statement recorded under Section 161, which is recorded in the presence of only the police and is not admissible as evidence in the court. The article claimed that the case against me was now watertight. But I feigned indifference even as my heart beat faster due to what Pragya had told me.

'People write a lot of things,' I said. 'Not all of it may be true.'

'Exactly,' she said. 'You wrote articles about me too. But do you really know what the truth is?'

I stood still, at a loss for words. All this time, I had written about her based on what I had heard, read or investigated. Now, I was on the receiving end from the media, and the most absurd reports were being written about me. I had begun to believe in the innocence of anyone in the jail who claimed to have been framed in the crimes they were accused of. Pragya seemed to sense the unease on my face.

'I know you haven't committed the crime,' she said. 'These bad times will pass.'

I just nodded and looked through the gaps into her room. It was remarkably clean and well maintained. Some of her clothes had been hung to dry over the clothes line in the passage. Her belongings were neatly organized. The bathrooms inside the cell had no doors. There was a tubelight in the room, and an earthen pot for storing drinking water. She also had a bed to sleep in, because she was suffering from severe back pain. There was also a *murti* of Lord Krishna, in his childhood avatar. She told me she did puja every day. Looking at the idol, I remembered how my grandmother too used to pray to Lord Krishna.

'All of this has been allowed by the court,' she said, referring to the concessions that were made available to her. 'And don't worry. Lord Krishna will guide you out of these troubled waters.'

The woman whom I had written against extensively was praying for my safety. I had reported every minute detail on her case, because I had a source in the team that was investigating the Malegaon blasts. Yet, she hadn't taken it personally. I thanked her for the prayers.

In many ways, this interaction planted the first seeds of spirituality in my heart, which I have pursued even after my release from jail. I felt a kind of solidarity towards Pragya.

Our destinies had indeed intertwined because there was another common denominator between us—ATS chief Hemant Karkare, who was killed in the 26/11 Mumbai terror attacks in 2008.

*

It was Wednesday, 26 November 2008, when Karkare called Megha Prasad, a reporter with Times Now, and me, to the ATS office at Nagpada. I had only known Karkare since the first press conference the ATS had conducted about the Malegaon blasts, and this was my third meeting with him. We made it just in time for the appointment at 4 p.m. Karkare was dressed in a sky-blue shirt and blue trousers. He did not operate with the flair of some of his other outspoken colleagues. He went about his business in a silent and effective manner. The alleged involvement of the right wing in the cases he was investigating had put him under considerable political pressure. Pragya had also levelled charges of extreme torture against the ATS, which had begun a political controversy.

Karkare ordered for three cups of tea as soon as we sat down.

'Sir,' Megha said. 'Any new developments in the Malegaon investigations that can be shared with the media?'

'Why are you asking me?' he laughed. 'Jigna should know better. I have been following Jigna's reports. She knows what has been going on in the investigation room. I wonder who in the ATS is providing her with such minute details.'

I smiled. 'The information seems to find its way to me, sir.'

He smiled in response—a way of telling me it was okay.

'But, sir,' I said, 'I haven't done a big story in the last two days. My editor is pushing me to get one.'

'Well, give my regards to Mr Zaidi,' he said. 'But Malegaon is a political landmine. I can't divulge more.'

As we finished drinking the tea, precisely at 4.35 p.m., he received a call from the office of R.R. Patil, the then home minister of Maharashtra. Karkare informed us that he would have to leave for the Mantralaya immediately to meet the home minister.

'But, sir,' I said. 'When can we get something to write about?'

'Meet me this Friday.' He smiled as he stood up. 'You'll get some big news to break.'

He accompanied us out of his office and walked with us to the exit. He got into the back seat of his official car and was driven away. I wondered about the big news he wanted to speak about, but my thoughts were broken by Megha's voice.

'Jigna,' she said. 'A new officer has joined as the additional commissioner, south region. Should we go and introduce ourselves?'

'Who is he?'

'Himanshu Roy,' she said. 'Earlier, he was posted as the commissioner of police, Nashik.'

'Not today,' I said. 'I have to report back to office.'

'Okay,' she said. 'Let's meet Mr Roy another day.'

Later in the day, I returned to the *Asian Age* office in Todi Industrial Estate at Lower Parel, and quickly filed my story for the day. I had to catch up with a friend for dinner at the Orchid Hotel in Andheri East. As I was getting ready to leave after discussing the next day's plan and some developments on the Malegaon story with Zaidi sir, a series of messages about a shoot-out at Leopold Café in Colaba came in.

'Don't leave till we know what's going on,' Zaidi sir said. 'It could be a gang war.' Soon, reports started coming in about the shoot-out at the Taj Mahal Hotel, at the Chhatrapati Shivaji Terminus (CST), and other places. What transpired later was the biggest terrorist strike on Mumbai. A well-planned effort to take the city hostage.

I can never forget the chaos, the news alerts and the images that flashed on the television. One of them was of Karkare putting on a bulletproof vest and headgear to counter the terrorists who had entered the state-run Cama and Albless Hospital, a few metres away from the CST.

At around 1 a.m., I received a call from a trusted source. He was the one who had been providing me nuggets of information from the Malegaon blast probe.

'Madam, Hemant Karkare sir is no more.'

'What?' I shrieked.

'Sahab was shot dead by the terrorists.'

Only a few hours ago, I had been sitting in Mr Karkare's cabin and sipping tea with him. And now, he had been martyred while fulfilling his duties. All of it came rushing back to me—his quiet manner, his sky-blue shirt, his promise about a big story. I rushed to Zaidi sir's cabin and broke the news, leaving him in shock. I also called Megha about Karkare's death.

'What are you saying?' she said, unable to believe her ears.

'Yes,' I said, my voice choking. 'Where are you?'

'I am covering the attack near Metro Junction. We just received some information about terrorists shooting at the cops. The terrorists are now driving towards Chowpatty.'

As reporters, we often keep our emotions in control even as we deal with traumatic topics. But news of Karkare's death had brought tears to my eyes.

I sobbed. Karkare had been inside a Toyota Qualis with other police officers and constables when the terrorists had attacked them. The terrorists then took the police vehicle and fled the spot.

'Are you sure about his death?' Megha asked. 'Should I break it on television?'

'Yes,' I said, still crying. 'The news is confirmed.'

And then I watched the news being played out on TV. Hemant Karkare had died protecting his nation in a small lane only a few metres away from the Crime Branch office. Two other officers, ACP Ashok Kamte and Senior Inspector Vijay Salaskar, had also been killed. The man who had arrested several alleged right-wing extremists was no more, and the big story he wanted to break had also been laid to rest with him.

*

Paromita spared no chance to boast about her considerable influence with the Intelligence Bureau (IB). She claimed to know that I had been framed in this case, and that I was going to be released soon. I had no clue if there was any truth in her words, but it disturbed me enough to discuss these things with my lawyer. As usual, he advised me to trust no one.

One night, as I was preparing to go to sleep, Paromita asked me about my interactions with Pragya.

'I think she is innocent,' I said.

'She told you that?' Paromita laughed. 'Quite a manipulator she is!'

'Why'd you say that?'

'Because she confessed about her involvement to me.'

I gasped. 'What?'

I had no clue who was speaking the truth. I was unsure why Paromita always kept a close eye on who was getting friendly with me. Perhaps, it was because Pragya was locked in a power struggle with the other powerful inmate in Byculla Jail—Jaya Chheda—and Paromita had chosen to side with Jaya. I did not want to be a part of these games.

'Jiggy,' Paromita said. 'Will you seek revenge against those who have wronged you?'

'Never thought about it,' I said and returned to my space. I turned over and tried to sleep.

After Paromita's warning, I kept away from Pragya as much as I could. The sadhvi called for me quite a few times, but I would excuse myself on some pretext or the other. Pragya had a court order that allowed her home-made food. She once sent across a portion of *undhiyu*, a popular Gujarati delicacy, for me, but I politely sent it back to her. A few days later, around 2.30 a.m., I woke up to the sounds of utensils clanging loudly inside the jail. Pragya was smashing her aluminium plate on the wall and creating a ruckus. The jail authorities arrived and made sure the situation was handled. The next morning, a group of women who had been arrested from Nagpur for alleged Naxal links began a hunger strike to protest against the quality of food in the jail. It turned out that the clanging of utensils had been a signal from Pragya to those women to begin the strike. The food remained the same however. But I learnt that Pragya would constantly work to keep jail authorities on their toes.

Every Friday, the jail superintendent would visit all the barracks. It was an important event and the barracks had to be cleaned by us on Thursdays so that the superintendent would be pleased. We scrubbed the floor with Ariel detergent. The superintendent would ask the inmates if they were facing any problems in the jail. But everyone kept mum because no corrective action was ever taken for any complaint or request. Moreover, the constables inside the jail would take it as a personal insult if an inmate complained, and they would make that inmate's life all the more miserable. The superintendent would always speak very politely to me.

Pragya, like everyone else, kept mum too. For her, initiating the strike was the way to make a point. She made it a point to celebrate all Hindu festivals. In March 2012, on the occasion of Holi, she brought her Lord Krishna idol outside her cell and performed an elaborate puja in the barrack. She also arranged for small sachets of *gulal*, and all the inmates celebrated Holi with her. That day, she tied a sacred thread around my wrist and put a pendant with an inscription of 'Om' around my neck. Even though I had kept my distance from her, I had no urge to stop her from tying the thread. She said she had performed a special prayer for my release, and for her prayers to be answered, it was important for me to keep the thread on my wrist until I was out of jail.

About a month later, Pragya was shifted to a Madhya Pradesh jail. Strangely, when I myself left the jail, the sacred thread she had given me came loose on my wrist, on its own.

5

FIRST ENCOUNTER
WITH THE POLICE

May 2004

I rushed down the busy streets of Ghatkopar with my neighbour to head for the Pant Nagar police station. Onlookers stared at me as if a mad woman had escaped from a mental asylum. My dishevelled hair flew all over my face. Sweat dripped down my neck. I was wearing a salwar kameez, but in the panic, I had forgotten to drape a dupatta. I had never visited a police station before and had to ask my neighbours for assistance. The uncle who lived next door was kind enough to help.

A week before, while I was at my husband's home in Gujarat, I had packed my bags and informed my in-laws that I was going on a vacation to my mother's place in Mumbai along with my son. He was four years old then, and his nursery school was closed for the summer vacations. I held him close during the lonely train journey back home. When I arrived in Mumbai, I told my grandfather that I had no intention to go back to live with my husband. My grandfather informed my mother-in-law over a phone call.

A few days later, my mother-in-law came down to my maternal home in Ghatkopar, accompanied by my sister-in-law, who lived in Mumbai. Our families met in the living room, and my in-laws seemed accommodating of my decision to separate. I was on friendly terms with my sister-in-law. She was emotionally attached to my son as well. So, when she asked if she could take my son downstairs for a walk, I saw no reason to deny her request. After twenty minutes, she sent word that she wanted to take him to her place in Wadala for two days. Again, I didn't see why she couldn't. In fact, I packed my son's clothes, and his favourite toy—a tiny yellow plastic autorickshaw—and kissed him goodbye.

But as soon as my in-laws left, I wondered if I had made a huge mistake. What if they used my son as a tool to pressurize me back into the marriage? What if they refused to give me custody of him? I was unsure if the divorce would be mutual or if it would turn ugly. Panicking with these terrible thoughts, I decided to approach the Mumbai Police. A complaint would maintain a record of the events that had occurred.

At the Pant Nagar police station, we approached the reception desk and asked about the procedure to file a complaint. A weary cop looked up from the police register and pointed towards a desk. The policeman at the desk asked what the complaint was about. I narrated the incident.

'Madam,' the cop said, 'if you allowed your sister-in-law to take the kid, we can't file a complaint. You can register a non-cognizable (NC) case.'

I agreed.

'But why do you not want to go back to your husband?' he asked.

'My husband is an alcoholic,' I said. 'He drinks at least one bottle every day. Then, he turns into a monster.'

'Where is your husband?'

'In Bharuch.'

'How can he drink, then?' the cop said in a deadpan manner. 'Not possible. Gujarat is under prohibition.'

'Ask anyone in Bharuch. The entire city knows how much he drinks.'

I married my husband on 4 December 1998. It was an arranged marriage. I had completed studying law from Ruparel College, and my parents thought it was the perfect time for me to settle down. I gave up an internship with a reputed law firm and married the man my parents had chosen for me. I was told my husband was an engineer and ran a printing press in Gujarat. But after we returned from a honeymoon in Kerala, I found his mark sheet in the cupboard while unpacking the suitcases. He had failed in the tenth standard. I felt cheated, but was convinced by my family to uphold the sanctity of my marital vows. What if my husband had lied? I was still supposed to treat him like a *parameshwar*.

Soon, my husband started restricting my interactions with my family. I wasn't allowed to meet my mother. My father had given them a brand new Indica car, on an agreement that my husband would make the car available for my father whenever he would visit India on a vacation from his workplace in Dubai. I never saw what the Indica looked like on the inside because my husband never allowed me to sit in it.

My father would call from Dubai every Thursday to check on me. In those days, the landline telephones would chime a longer ring than usual for ISD calls. As soon as my husband would hear that long ring, he would throw the handset at my face and say, '*Tere baap ka phone aaya hai.*' Those rings evoked such fear inside me that I would mute the ringer around the time my father would usually call. I even forbade my mother to call me while my husband was at home. My husband and in-laws sold all of the 100 *tola* of gold I had received from my parents and relatives as gifts within the first three months of my marriage.

I was not allowed to go out of the house alone or socialize—my sister-in-law or mother-in-law would always accompany me. This ploy ensured I would not reveal my troubled married life to others in the community. I was confined to the house and did all the work in the kitchen.

I was nothing more than a maid in that house. I wasn't even allowed to read English newspapers.

Very early into the marriage, I conceived for the first time. Walking out of the marriage was all the more improbable now. In September 1999, I gave birth to a very beautiful baby girl, whom we named Sanjana. The girl was only thirty days old when a terrible fever engulfed her. Her stomach bloated inordinately. We rushed her to a hospital in Bharuch but the lack of good medical facilities forced us to shift the baby to a better hospital in Surat. The girl was in a lot of pain, and the medical treatment left puncture wounds all over her body. Despite our best efforts, she succumbed on 19 October. The cause of death was said to be septicaemia.

I thought this terrible incident would change my husband, but his alcoholism continued unabated. He would drink when his business suffered losses. He would drink in times of happiness, on festivals like Diwali. I started fearing all festivals because my husband would call a horde of friends and I would have to cook dinner for all the men as they enjoyed their drinks and snacks. My husband did not even realize how many of his drunk friends leered at me.

In December 1999, my father-in-law was diagnosed with last-stage cancer. He would often climb the stairs to the first floor, and knock on my bedroom in the middle of the night and request to be taken to the bathroom. I did all I could for him because he was the only one who treated me well. He often counselled my husband to stop misbehaving with me. He was the father figure I had missed growing up. But he passed away on 9 February 2000, and I lost the only person I cared for in that house. We cremated him in Nasik.

A few months later, I conceived again. My blood group is A–, and my husband was AB+. My mother-in-law was convinced that the 'negativity' of my blood group had caused my daughter's death. My husband seemed to agree with his mother and taunted me endlessly. They subjected me to such mental trauma that I started to believe this would turn into a self-fulfilling prophecy of sorts. What if my second child met the same fate as my first? I did not want to put another child, and even myself, through such physical and mental pain again. I decided to undergo a thorough medical examination in Mumbai. My husband accompanied me. The test reports from a maternity home near my place in Ghatkopar proved that there was nothing wrong with my blood type, and I had even been given Rh injections. The doctor said that my baby daughter had most likely contracted an external infection. I convinced my husband to get tested too. His medical reports suggested that the survival of a girl child between us would be extremely precarious on account of a chromosomal abnormality in him. I was just four weeks pregnant. Sex determination had legal ramifications. The doctor suggested that medical treatment could help in this situation.

In the fifth month of my pregnancy, I developed severe pain in my stomach. My cervix was under pressure from the baby's weight, and I had to be immediately hospitalized. I spent many days in the hospital, and after I was discharged I was recommended complete bed rest. This was not possible at my in-laws' place as I was as good as a maid there. My mother-in-law decided to send me back to my maternal home. Not out of concern or love, but to ensure that they would not have to take the fall should something go wrong again. If I was with my parents, any unfortunate incident would be solely my responsibility.

But with the blessings of Lord Krishna, I gave birth to a healthy boy in August 2000.

I hoped that a son would make my husband happy and improve my equation with my in-laws. But my hopes were dashed soon. Things only got worse, and I continued to endure, now for the sake of my child. The following year, my husband got so drunk on Holi that he urinated on our bed thinking it was the toilet.

As my son began learning his first words, he also picked up the abuses my husband hurled at me with regular abandon. When he was four, I scolded him one day for misbehaving. His expression completely matched his father's when he said, *'Chal nikal ja ghar se!'* Tears flowed down my cheeks. It wasn't his fault that he was living in such an environment. But if this continued, he would grow up to be like his father and treat other women the same way I was being treated now. I couldn't let that happen. We had to leave. I packed our bags and walked out of an irreparable marriage, for good.

The policeman at Pant Nagar police station showed little emotion as he heard my tale, and took down the NC report. The entire process took two harrowing hours and I returned home. The next day, my sister-in-law called and listened to my concerns. Her fiancé called me from Australia and tried to tell me that my son could have a good future in Australia. I was furious and demanded that I wanted my son back home in the next hour. My sister-in-law eventually dropped off my son at my building. She did not come up to my door.

My divorce was settled mutually. I did not ask for any alimony. My husband promised he would return 100 tolas of gold in reasonable time. That never happened.

Slowly, I started picking up the shattered pieces of my life and also arranged my son's admission to a school. A law internship for me was out of the question. My earlier stint with a law firm had not paid enough to sustain a thirty-one-year-old single mother and her child.

I researched a few career options and settled on the media. I joined a one-year evening diploma course at Somaiya College, which was close to my home. I made sure my son went to school in the morning, and in the evening, while he would play with his friends, and his grandparents would look after him, I would attend college. Velly Thevar, my faculty at Somaiya, was a well-known crime reporter working for the *Times of India*. Her lectures sparked my interest in crime reporting and I began to idolize her. She often said that the *Free Press Journal* (FPJ) was the best place to start a career in journalism.

As a result, I started reading the *Free Press Journal*. In a matter of days, I saw an advertisement in the paper that they needed trainee reporters. Mr Singh interviewed me at the *FPJ* office in Nariman Point. The sprawling view of the city from his cabin enthralled me. The editor asked me to join from 19 November 2005, at a salary of Rs 3,000 per month. Lack of any experience meant I couldn't be a crime reporter yet. So, they assigned me to court reporting.

My first assignment was to cover gangster Abu Salem's case at the TADA court situated inside Arthur Road Jail. Ujjwal Nikam, the public prosecutor, opened his statement with a Sanskrit shloka to demand custody of Abu Salem. I noted the measured movements of his hands, the command of his voice and the choice of words, and covered it all in an article that made it to the front page of the *Free Press Journal*. It was my first byline too, a term I was unaware of until then. Ujjwal Nikam personally called to congratulate me on a well-written report.

I would travel in the second-class compartment in the local trains, pursue leads at the sessions court, file my stories, and rush back home to be with my son. My course at Somaiya College suffered, but for good performance at work, my salary at *FPJ* was increased to Rs 5,000 in the following month. In ten months, my salary touched Rs 7,500. Things were finally beginning to look up.

6

RULER OF THE JAIL

I counted each day spent in jail. Days had turned into months and it caused turmoil within me. In the first two months, Paromita protected me from a lot of trouble. She stood up if someone tried to misbehave. She warned me in case someone tried to hoodwink me. She was always there. The other inmates always discussed Paromita's sexual preferences, but it didn't bother me.

It was mid-January when Paromita and I were chatting over a tasteless plate of *poha* in the morning when she first mentioned Jaya Chheda.

'Jaya Maa is coming back from the hospital,' she said. 'You've heard of her.'

'Oh yes. Of course, I have,' I replied.

Jaya Chheda was the ex-wife of Suresh Bhagat, Mumbai's *matka* king who had a thriving 3,000-crore-rupee business. Jaya, known for her aggression, and her son Hitesh were being tried for murdering Bhagat in an orchestrated road accident. A speeding truck had rammed straight into his SUV, mowing it down to pieces, and all the occupants had died. It was proved in court to be a well-thought-out plan to gain control over the vast gambling business that Bhagat had inherited from his father and grown.

'Jaya Maa is very powerful,' Paromita said. 'Not a leaf moves inside Byculla Jail without her consent.'

'Really?'

'Yes,' she said. 'She is away, on a vacation at the Saifee Hospital.'

'Vacation?'

'What else do you call a long stay at an air-conditioned room in a private hospital?'

Jaya had always been on the heavier side. Before being imprisoned at the Byculla Jail in 2008, she had undergone a bariatric surgery, called sleeve gastrectomy. The procedure involved surgical removal of a part of her stomach to reduce its size. The weight loss surgery ensured that she ate only a little, but it came with the risk of food leaking out of the tube. If she ate a type and amount of food that was not permitted, it would cause severe complications. Jaya used this to her benefit and she would hop from one hospital to another while she was at the Byculla Jail.

Paromita commanded a lot of authority in the jail. But she spoke of Jaya with the reverence of a demigod, and this unnerved me. As a reporter I had a history with Jaya, which I made Paromita aware of. During my stint in *Mid-Day* in

2008, I was approached by a lawyer who worked for well-known advocate Harshad Ponda. The lawyer asked me if I was interested in a good story.

'About what?' I asked him.

'Our client, Suresh Bhagat, fears that his ex-wife is hatching a conspiracy for his murder,' the lawyer said. 'He recently wrote to the Mumbai Police seeking protection.'

'How can I help?'

'The police are hatching eggs over his application,' the lawyer said. 'Bhagat plans to file an application in the Bombay High Court.'

'So,' I said. 'A story in the newspapers will help his cause?'

The lawyer nodded. From his black robe, he pulled out a white envelope. It contained a copy of the application to be filed in the court. Inside, there was also a photograph of an overweight woman in a swimming pool, in the arms of a bare-chested man.

'Who is this woman?' I asked.

'Jaya Chheda, the ex-wife of my client,' the lawyer said. 'They divorced four years ago.'

'And the man?'

'He is Suhas Roge,' the lawyer said. 'Apparently, in a relationship with Jaya Chheda. He is playing his part in the conspiracy.' Roge was a member of the gang of Arun Gawli. Gawli, just about 5 ft 2 in tall, was an underworld Maharashtrian gangster-turned-politician who used to operate his gang from his home in Dagdi Chawl on Saat

Rasta in Byculla. Gawli had created his own place in the underworld by running extortion rackets and trade unions, among other things.

'Okay.' I folded the envelope into my purse. 'I'll think it over.'

When I returned home that day, I put the envelope into one of the cabinets above my writing desk, where I stored many important documents. I didn't pursue the story as it looked like it would be pushing Bhagat's agenda. Bhagat himself was no saint, and I had no way of making sure he was speaking the truth. Even if I had his court application, I had an inkling that there could be some agenda behind it. So, I left the story on the back burner.

In March 2008, I joined the *Asian Age*. On 13 June 2008, about six months after my meeting with the lawyer, Bhagat died in a ghastly road accident on the Alibaug–Pen road. He was returning after attending a hearing in Alibaug court in a 1997 narcotics case. As his Scorpio jeep reached the Dharamtar Bridge, it had a head-on collision with a truck. All seven occupants of the SUV, including Bhagat, died in the fatal collision. The lawyer who had met me died too.

As soon as I heard the news of Bhagat's death, I ran to my editor Hussain Zaidi's cabin to tell him about my meeting with the lawyer. I was suspicious about Bhagat's sudden death and told Zaidi sir that there could be more behind the accident. He advised me to keep the document and the photograph handy in case the investigation developed some new angle. He also asked me to confirm the identity of the man who was in the photograph with Jaya Chheda.

I went home and found the envelope between two stapled stacks of papers. My next task was to confirm Roge's identity. The next day I carried the photograph to the office of Rakesh Maria, who was then the joint commissioner, Crime Branch, and explained the purpose of my visit. The tall, lean man who had broken hardened criminals with his clinical interrogations leaned forward in his chair, resting his elbows on the centre of his desk. He balanced the frame of his spectacles perfectly along the bridge of his nose and considered the audacity of my request.

I placed the photograph on his desk. 'Is this Suhas Roge?'

He cast a cursory glance at the photograph and looked away. For a moment, his face gave away nothing. Then he stared at me in his ice-cool demeanour, and leaned back into his chair, and paused in a measured manner before he nodded his head, only once. That was all the assurance I needed, and I called Zaidi sir on the way back to the office to confirm that the man in the photograph was Roge indeed. There were already murmurs about investigators considering the angle of foul play in Bhagat's death. I extracted more from my sources in the Crime Branch and it turned out that they were already probing Roge's role in the accident along with Jaya Chheda.

The same week, we ran a front-page exclusive story about the Crime Branch's suspicion and Bhagat's fear of a life threat that the cops had not taken seriously. With my story, we ran the exclusive photograph of Jaya and Roge posing together happily in the pool. A few weeks after I broke the story, the police arrested eight people for Bhagat's murder, including Jaya, her son Hitesh and her alleged lover Roge.

I told Paromita about the story I had written on Jaya in great detail. Despite my lawyer's reservations about sharing stories about my past with other inmates, I had grown close to Paromita and had begun to trust her a little, though I couldn't trust her wholeheartedly. When she heard about my history with Jaya, a worried expression descended upon her face.

'Will Jaya remember I wrote a front-page article against her?' I asked.

'Jaya Maa never forgives,' Paromita said. 'And she never forgets.'

'What should I do then?'

'Don't worry,' she said. 'I'll set things right.'

I mentally steeled myself. I worried until I realized I had nothing more to lose. What more could she put me through? That thought gave me a sense of fearlessness, but I didn't relay this to Paromita.

One monotonous night at the end of January 2012, I had grown bored of watching Doordarshan and retired to my space around 9.30 p.m., preparing to sleep. I had a clear view of the entrance, and in the dim light, I saw Jaya walking down the veranda wearing a crisp, peach-coloured dress. She had lost weight due to the bariatric surgery, but she was unmistakably recognizable from the swagger in her stride. She was a short woman in her fifties, but not a single strand of white was visible in her dyed black hair. She crossed over to Barrack No. 1, which was a common barrack reserved for inmates who arrived in jail after the evening headcount so that they could be repatriated to their assigned barracks in the morning. In a world where others used their clothes as makeshift pillows, Jaya had the privilege of using a thick mattress, a fluffy cotton pillow and even a quilt; all of which had been moved to Barrack No. 1 for her impending arrival. The way she looked around it seemed like she was the queen of the jail.

The next morning, after breakfast, a large group of women queued up outside Barrack No. 1. Hardened inmates bowed at Jaya's feet as if she was the high priestess of a holy land. Usha Maa, the warden who had been jailed for scheming with her lover to kill her husband, made a special visit from Barrack No. 5 to pay her respects. Paromita grabbed my arm and asked me to come along to greet Jaya Maa. Politely, I excused myself and assured her that I would go when the time was right. Paromita seemed to understand. From a safe distance, I saw her bow down to Jaya Maa. Paromita hugged her tight, and she reciprocated, a little too closely I thought.

Over the next few days, many of the people under trial, including Tania, stopped talking to me, especially when

Jaya was around. A few months before my arrest, Tania had given birth to a daughter in jail, whom the inmates had named Duggu. After Jaya came back from the hospital, Tania would get very uncomfortable if I got anywhere close to the child. One day, when Jaya was out on a court visit, I asked Tania about the change in her demeanour. She sought my forgiveness but made it clear that inside Byculla Jail, upsetting Jaya Maa was a cardinal sin she couldn't afford to commit. The court was hearing Jaya's case on a regular basis, but I remained wary of the days she did not have a court visit scheduled. I made conscious efforts to avoid 'her' areas. It was my way of staying out of trouble.

Jaya was a shrewd manipulator. Because of her weight loss surgery, she could barely eat. She had managed to get a court order issued that allowed her delivery of home-cooked food, three times a day. Edible food was a rarity inside Byculla Jail, but Jaya received multi-tiered tiffin boxes every single day, filled with hot chapatis, basmati rice, dal tadka, various types of curries, pickle and salad. Clean drinking water was a scarce commodity, but Jaya could arrange bottles of Bisleri and cans of fruit juice. She could even arrange pizza from Domino's if she pleased. Like the ruler of her fiefdom, she distributed her food to the less privileged undertrials and won over the undying loyalty of many hungry women. Eventually, Paromita again asked me to pay my obeisance to Jaya Maa. She assured me that Jaya would not harm me. Running out of time and excuses, I played along.

When I approached her, Jaya showed no upfront signs of hostility and offered me a bowl of *aam ras* laced with saffron. I had grown up in a Gujarati household where mango pulp was a staple for breakfast during the mango season. Tempted, I reached for the pulp, but realized my mistake and pulled back. Jaya coaxed me with a smile, and I gave in. I scooped up a spoonful, and it was the finest Alphonso pulp I had tasted in my life—in Byculla Jail of all places. Jaya smiled with the calmness of a god, as if she had bestowed a favour and turned a sceptic into a believer.

'Mahale arrested you?' she asked, in her Kutch dialect.

'Yes.'

'I can get you out in no time.'

'Really?'

'Yes,' she said. 'First, we'll get them to drop the MCOCA charges.'

I tried to appear impressed, answering in Gujarati and humouring her brouhaha. Senior Inspector Ramesh Mahale was also responsible for Jaya's arrest, and all her talk of being able to get me out was nothing but a cock and bull story. If that were true, why was she still in jail? But ticking off Jaya would be the wrong move inside the walls of Byculla Jail. I tactfully displayed my acceptance of her superiority by making her feel she ruled the place, and she appeared pleased by the end of our conversation.

*

Two days later, a huge commotion broke out inside the barracks. Inmates banged their aluminium mugs on the walls, screaming and shouting. They refused to queue up for breakfast. I asked Paromita what the fuss was all about.

'The inmates are going on a hunger strike,' she said.

'Hunger strike? Why?'

'To protest against the strip search.'

'Huh?'

Paromita whispered into my ear. 'Jaya Maa was strip-searched when she returned from a court visit. She has instigated them.'

'Should I join?' I asked, with no intention of doing so.

'No,' she said. 'Stay away.'

The jailer arrived and quoted the rules and the manuals of the strip search procedure. The inmates protested with all their might, but the strike fizzled out by the evening. The rest of the day, I kept to my corner and chanted the *Hanuman Chalisa*, a practice I had been following for a while. Clearly, Jaya thought she could get away with anything.

Around the same time, my lawyer obtained an order from the court for getting home-cooked food delivered to me, but only one tiffin box a day was granted. My cousin would deliver it to jail in the morning. With no refrigeration, the food would become inedible by afternoon. After opting for home-cooked food, I was also no longer eligible for my portion of the food served in jail. Paromita would share her dinner with me, but I could not bear the guilt of eating from her plate and feeding myself. So, I started going hungry to bed.

Also, as much as my family loved me, travelling daily from Ghatkopar to Byculla was no easy arrangement for people who had jobs and businesses to attend to, and bills to pay. I asked my lawyer to put in an application in court for cancelling the home food order. The judge was aghast that an undertrial wanted to eat the food served in jail, but the order was finally rescinded. I had three square meals to eat again.

The African undertrials, with an enormous amount of strength, acted like hired guns for Jaya. Jaya would often use the Africans to send across a message to other inmates and warn them off from acting against her. Jaya would never directly say anything to an inmate, but she liked to show her strength through the Africans. They had turned into mercenaries, all for the want of good food. Jaya could not bear it if any other inmate was revered. She still held a grudge against me for writing those stories against her, and especially for publishing her photo along with Roge. So, there was no way I could be in her good books. Behind that angelic smile on her round face, she was a master strategist, who could get what she wanted without getting her hands dirty. Inside the prison walls, there existed only one mantra for survival: J for Jail, J for Jaya.

7

JOINING *MUMBAI MIRROR*

After ten months in the *Free Press Journal*, I started looking for another job. A colleague in *FPJ* had moved to *Mumbai Mirror*, and he asked if I was interested in joining the newspaper as a court reporter.

Mumbai Mirror had launched with a bang. On 29 May 2005, a day before its first issue was published, actor Abhishek Bachchan and the then chief minister Vilasrao Deshmukh had launched the compact newspaper at the Gateway of India in an elaborate ceremony. The fireworks, laser shows and lighting unveiled the red-and-black *Mumbai Mirror* logo in the south Mumbai sky. The tabloid's launch also marked the city's most aggressive print rivalry. *Mid-Day* was already popular in the tabloid space and there were two new broadsheets coming up—*Daily News and Analysis* (*DNA*) and a Mumbai edition of *Hindustan Times*. There was a sudden spurt in journalism jobs. It was a good time to be in journalism as reporters were poached at almost 80–100 per cent salary hikes by rival newspapers. *Mumbai Mirror*'s editor, Meenal Baghel, too was poached from *Mid-Day*, along with many other reporters.

I quickly sent in my résumé and was called for an interview. The visit to the *Times of India* building at Fort, opposite CST, was like a dream come true. A journalist reveres that building as much as a cricketer reveres the Lord's cricket ground at London. The *Mumbai Mirror* office was on the fourth floor. C. Unnikrishnan, the city editor of *Mumbai Mirror*, conducted the first round of interview. A few days later, I was called for a second round. I sat in front of Meenal Baghel, who interviewed me inside her carpeted cabin with wooden interiors. I had less than a year of experience in journalism. Meenal asked if I would be able to deliver 'page-one' stories—sensational, front-page, exclusive stories that became the talking point of the day was *Mumbai Mirror*'s USP. An exclusive for *Mumbai Mirror* meant that the story should not be in any other newspaper, not even in the *Times of India*.

'But *Mumbai Mirror* and *Times of India* are part of the same group?' I asked.

Meenal reiterated her stance on exclusivity and asked me to expect a call from HR. Over the next few days, I waited anxiously for the phone to ring. When I did get the call, I could not believe my ears when the HR offered me a salary of Rs 16,000 a month. That was about twice of what I was making in *FPJ*. I filled up forms for a new bank account and was sent for a medical check-up near the Breach Candy Hospital. I joined *Mumbai Mirror* just around the time when the tabloid celebrated its first anniversary. On my first day, the office was abuzz with gossip from the anniversary party. Coming from a conservative family, it was new for me to see female reporters smoking openly in the smoking bays. I could barely walk to the coffee vending machine in the corner of the office with confidence. *FPJ* was a small, informal set-up of five to six reporters. Though one of the best places to learn, it hadn't prepared me to mingle in a large corporate office. *Mumbai Mirror* had a much bigger team. There were a city team, crime team, features team, and a battery of news editors and designers. I was excited as well as intimidated.

I had stumbled upon a good story while serving my notice period at *FPJ*. I had decided to work on it after joining the *Mumbai Mirror*. I wanted to deliver a page-one story as early as possible. The story was about a man named Arif Lakdawala, who owned a petrol pump near Pydhonie. Lakdawala was wanted as a witness at the Sara Sahara trial. Iqbal Kaskar, the brother of fugitive don Dawood Ibrahim, was an accused in this case. The court was summoning Lakdawala for deposition. But he was seemingly untraceable as per records, even though he was very much in the city. I discussed the story with Meenal and she thought it was a page one. But she wouldn't accept the story unless I had a photograph of Lakdawala.

'How do I get his photograph?' I asked Meenal. 'I have never visited the shady areas around Dongri all my life.'

'No photograph, no story,' Meenal said. 'Take a photographer along. Get a good picture.'

I sighed. I found the address of the petrol pump from the court documents. By late evening, I reached the place along with the photographer. I asked the photographer to keep a safe distance from the petrol pump and click the photo at the first opportunity. 'Call for help if I don't come back in fifteen minutes,' I said, and walked to the petrol pump.

Though situated in the midst of a bustling area, the petrol pump was dark and seedy. Three men were sitting on plastic chairs, discussing something in low voices.

'Is Arif Bhai here?' I asked.

They looked up at me suspiciously. I gulped before one of them eventually replied that *bhaijaan* would arrive in fifteen minutes. I waited. Across the street, the photographer was trying to blend into the crowd. I called him up and spoke in a low whisper. 'Arif will be here soon. Click the photograph at the first opportunity.'

Arif Lakdawala arrived wearing a cream-coloured *pathani* suit. He was tall, in his mid-forties, and sported a moustache. My heart thudded loud as I walked up to him and introduced myself as a reporter from *Mumbai Mirror*, though I did not reveal I was doing a story on him. 'Why are you not showing up in court despite multiple summons?' I asked.

He appeared amused, and from the corner of my eye, I saw the photographer clicking a few shots. Lakdawala did not bother answering me. Before I could get into trouble, I ended the conversation and rushed out as fast as I could without turning around to look at him. Back at the office, Meenal okayed the photograph. It was my third day in *Mumbai Mirror*, and I had delivered a page-one story.

Next morning, my phone didn't stop ringing. Television reporters wanted to follow up on the story and wanted more details. At the office, Unnikrishnan congratulated me for the fabulous start. Meenal too appreciated the good work. I was on cloud nine. It was then that I met Hussain Zaidi for the first time. He was heading the crime team at *Mumbai Mirror*.

'Oh, so you are Jigna Vora?' he said with a sarcastic smile on his face. Perhaps, the veteran in him had sensed that I might be driving recklessly in the fast lane. 'The Arif Lakdawala story is creating a lot of ripples.'

The next day, Iqbal Mamdani, a reporter with India TV, called me. 'Do you have a death wish?' he asked.

When I asked for a clarification, he informed me that Arif had called him and threatened to file a defamation case against me and my organization. I got jittery. I would even make sure to check no one was following me during my daily commute. But the fear wore off after a few days.

The sessions court at Kala Ghoda, opposite Jehangir Art Gallery—where, ironically, my trial would be held years later—was my assigned beat. I would take a train from

Ghatkopar to CST, and then take a bus to the sessions court. The court campus had an old building, and a new building with five floors. There were fifty-eight courtrooms in the entire complex. *Mumbai Mirror* had taught me to look at the peculiar details in stories, be it a new story being reported for the first time or an ongoing development that could have an edgy, unusual angle to it. Within the next few days, I wrote a story on the various tricks that the prosecution employed to prolong trials. The judges would merely impose fines ranging from Rs 20 to Rs 200. The story had a very catchy headline: *'Tareekh pe tareekh'*.

After spending 4–5 hours every day in the court premises, I would return to the *Times of India* building around 4 p.m. Gradually, I started interacting with many accused and known criminals in the court. For me, the line between court reporting and crime reporting slowly began to blur. One day I found out that Iqbal Kaskar had made an application in court to get his meals from home because the potatoes served in jail resulted in an allergic reaction, which led to itching. This would not be a worthy story in the minds of many, but for a tabloid, Dawood's brother feeling itchy due to the potatoes served in jail was a fun story that made it to page one.

In 1993, I covered the bomb blast trials meticulously. Once, Yakub Memon shouted in court that the CBI had failed to adhere to the terms under which the Memon family had agreed to return to India. This apparently included a pact that women would not be punished.

64

Yakub's wife had been acquitted, but Rubina Memon, his sister-in-law, was convicted because a car used in the bombings had been registered in her name. Yakub wanted to point out that his sister-in-law was unaware that her husband had purchased a car in her name. Subsequently, Suleiman Memon, Rubina's husband and Yakub's brother, was acquitted. I reported all the developments in this case.

In 2007, I met Sanjay Dutt several times during his trial. He spoke to me in fluent Gujarati. 'You speak Gujarati better than I do,' I would tell him. Once, he winked and replied that he had had to impress a Gujarati co-star early in his career. Learning her language seemed the best way to go about it. Dutt wore the same pair of stylish shoes for most of the trial. The reporter in me was curious if they'd make a story. Like a fool, I asked him where he had purchased the shoes from.

'Bangkok,' he replied.

I could not resist asking him, 'How much?'

He rattled off an absurdly high figure, and I nearly fainted. He would always chew tiny mints and offer me some. I took a liking to the strong flavour.

'Where do you get this mint?' I asked.

'Abroad, mostly,' he said. 'But you can get them in Bandra. I'll arrange for you?' I thanked him and decided to find them myself. I scoured Bandra for three days until I found the mints in an imported chocolate shop near a popular eatery.

Sanju Baba was funny at times. He once joked that he used Bacardi for mouthwash. I still remember the day of his judgment. I was in court when O.P. Chatwal, who was then a superintendent of police with the Central Bureau of Investigation (CBI), received a call and attended to it away from the public glare. He returned and whispered something in Ujjwal Nikam's ear. Nikam, the public prosecutor, toned down considerably while demanding the quantum of punishment to be given to Sanjay Dutt. And that was my story. Who was Chatwal's mystery caller? Sanjay was shivering and sweating during that hearing. He pleaded with the judge to be able to speak with his daughter once. The image of such a towering personality under so much stress remains entrenched in my memory to this day.

Another story that I cannot forget and will probably haunt me for ever is of Chhota Rajan's wife, Sujata Nikhalje. In December 2005, Sujata was arrested for extortion threats against a builder under the dreaded MCOCA. It was my first underworld story, and revealed the transcript of a conversation between Chhota Rajan and his wife where the don was missing his youngest daughter.

Once, my colleague Yogesh Sadhwani called early morning to give me a tip. A taxi driver had filed a complaint at Shivaji Park police station that three suspicious people, including a woman, had booked his taxi and conducted a recce of prominent spots like Haji Ali, Nariman Point and Shivaji Park. From their whispers, he feared that they were planning a terrorist attack. Now, the police were patrolling these areas day and night to prevent any untoward incident.

'See if you can find anything more,' Yogesh said and hung up.

I got in touch with a trusted source who confirmed that the news was true. My source called me to Haji Ali if I wanted more details. The source had sketches of the three suspected terrorists that the police had come up with based on the taxi driver's descriptions. The person requested that I not quote him in the story. I agreed and switched on the Bluetooth on my Nokia phone to exchange the sketches, with the waves lashing behind us. Next morning, I walked all the way to Ghatkopar railway station to check the first print of my newspaper at 4 a.m. The sketches were on the front page.

K.L. Prasad, then joint commissioner, law and order, flew into a rage. He had reportedly dressed down his boys, who he claimed had betrayed him and caused a security threat. The police called a press conference and referred to my story, which was then used by every television channel and newspaper in the city. I did not attend the press conference because I was worried. Even my source had no idea that the photographs would create such a storm.

I also distinctly remember reporting on the serial killer whom everyone was calling Beer Man. He left bottles of beer next to dead bodies after murdering them on the streets as his 'signature'. During that time, it happened that one night Meenal, our editor, was going hammer and tongs at all of us because there was no page-one story for the next morning's edition. I hadn't told her that I had been following up on a lead all day, because I was unsure if it would materialize. Unit One of the Crime Branch had conducted a kind of psychoanalysis and predicted the area in which the Beer Man would strike next. Around 9.30 p.m., my source called to inform that he was near the *TOI* building. I rushed downstairs to meet him, and he handed over the report that the police had come up with. There was no photograph to accompany this story, so one of our visual designers produced a well-drawn map. The story made it to the front page. Over the next few days, the Beer Man struck where the police had predicted.

I had become a regular page-one reporter despite covering the court beat. I must have delivered more than forty big stories in a year. From Abu Salem's biryani feast in jail to Pramod Mahajan's murder, a female judge's request to get Z-category security to inspect the Sara Sahara premises and the likely deportation of twelve criminals associated with Dawood and Chhota Shakeel, I worked hard to get big stories.

But when the annual appraisal came, I got a monthly increment of merely Rs 2,000. So I put in my papers. Meenal offered me a higher designation, but she was bound by the corporate slabs when it came to the monetary aspect.

I had an offer from the Press Trust of India, the country's largest news agency, which I brazenly used to bargain for a better offer from *Mid-Day*.

Meenal dissuaded me from joining *Mid-Day*. 'You'll never get the limelight that you're getting here,' she said. *Mid-Day* had offered me the position of a senior correspondent at a salary of Rs 35,000. How could I say no? And as luck would have it, I had a lead to a big story about encounter specialist Pradeep Sharma. I decided to keep the story in my bank and use it at the start of my stint with *Mid-Day*.

8

USHA MAA

From the corner of my eye, I saw Usha Maa, the warden, drying her waist-length hair. This plump and fair woman in her mid-fifties was a native of Uttar Pradesh. She was the only convict in Byculla Jail. All others were undertrials. She had draped the thin, yellow saree provided by the jail authorities quite low down on her waist. Her white blouse fit tightly over her arms. She must have been quite beautiful in her prime. She noticed I was looking, and started telling me how the hair was falling because of the jail water. I told her I was losing a lot of hair too.

'Get two bottles of Sesa Oil,' she said. 'That'll help.'

'Why two?' I asked.

'One for you,' she said. 'And one for me.'

I had no intention of getting into her bad books by not agreeing to her demand for a bottle of oil. A few days later, my cousin brought two bottles of Sesa Oil during the visiting hour. Usha Maa looked visibly happy. The oil did help stem my hairfall a bit too.

'Why were you arrested?' I asked Usha Maa.

She responded with a bizarre theory. Apparently, she lived in Juhu and was a regular visitor to the temple that was patronized by music baron Gulshan Kumar. She claimed to be a witness of Gulshan Kumar's murder near the temple and said she could identify the killers, who were allegedly Abu Salem's men. She said her husband worked for a rival gang and was murdered in a separate incident, but the police had implicated her in her husband's murder case due to his inter-gang rivalry with Salem's gang. None of it made sense. It sounded like a made-up story, but she said it all in such a convincing manner that it made me wonder if there was any truth to it.

Paromita had a different take on Usha Maa's case. According to her version, Usha Maa's husband owned a dairy farm near Jogeshwari. The man had happened to catch his wife with her lover in the haystacks of the cowshed. The husband was then found murdered, and this had led to Usha Maa's arrest and conviction.

As the warden, Usha Maa would order all inmates to clean the barracks, the toilet and the bathrooms on Thursdays to impress the superintendent the next day. Her voice could shake the walls of the jail. Influential prisoners like Jaya Chheda were exempt from such work. All inmates had to purchase one sachet of Surf washing powder with their own money for the cleaning. This was an unwritten rule. Due to the fascination that most of the prisoners had with me, I had acquired a celebrity-like status. So, I was never pushed for this task, but I wanted to kill time so badly that I happily volunteered for it every week. The two hours of washing and cleaning would keep me busy. The inmates would also have a little bit of fun by throwing bubbles of soap at each other and slipping on the surfaces. We would all be laughing until Usha Maa's thunderous voice would boom across the walls of the jail.

'*Ae randi*s!' she would scream. 'Get back to work!'

I wonder if Usha Maa knew anybody's name inside the jail because she addressed everybody with different words that ended up translating into 'prostitute'. The first time she had seen me, she had used the same phrase for me. But after she came to know more about me, her salutations changed. Once, I asked her why she addressed every woman that way. She rationalized that she'd been put through the same thing, and she was only passing it on as a tradition. Though I never agreed with her use of foul language, I could understand her frustration. More than seventeen years in prison could turn a woman's heart into stone.

Byculla wasn't even a women's prison back when Usha Maa was arrested. She was first sent to Arthur Road Jail and subsequently to other jails in the state over the seventeen years of her incarceration. A life sentence is generally fourteen years in prison, but even after completing this term, the convict's release papers are sent to various departments in the government, which can easily add a few more years to the process if the convict does not have the legal and family support to keep the files moving. Usha Maa's in-laws had already turned against her due to the nature of the case. She had two sons who rarely visited her. In fact, I never saw anyone come to meet her in the nine months I spent in jail. But Usha Maa was still hopeful of securing a release, like so many others. Jaya Chheda also raised Usha Maa's hopes by promising her legal and financial support. In her life as a prisoner, Usha Maa had seen so many prisoners secure bail, or be released, but she was still languishing. She would thus vent her frustration on the inmates.

Usha Maa was the link between the authorities and the inmates. I had more easy access to the authorities on account of my profession and education, but those lower down the order—beggars, robbers, drug peddlers, etc.— did not have this privilege. The solutions to their problems were determined by their personal equations with Usha Maa, and so they obeyed every command she issued.

Usha Maa also supervised the distribution of food. Fatima and other inmates would do the actual distribution. People would line up on the porch with aluminium plates in their hands and collect their food under her watchful eyes.

Anyone who helped Usha Maa with money or brought snacks for her from the canteen was a 'good woman' in her books, and Usha Maa praised them. I did not see anyone in Usha Maa's family ever send her a money order. The better-off inmates like Sujata Nikhalje or Jaya Chheda would buy biscuits and other items for Usha Maa and then extract favours in return. Usha Maa would also get other streetwise inmates like Fatima to smuggle packets of Manikchand gutkha into jail. Once, Usha Maa asked me to get a packet of henna to dye her hair on the way back from court. I was apprehensive because the constables wouldn't allow such items inside the jail.

'Don't worry,' Usha Maa said. 'You'll face no trouble getting it inside. I will talk to our randi constables,' said Usha Maa.

Usha Maa would regale others with her stories when she was in the mood for a conversation. In one such incident, a few years ago, a prostitute was arrested by the police and brought to Byculla Jail. Overnight, news of the prostitute's beauty spread like a wildfire. Next morning, Usha Maa visited Barrack No. 1 to take a look at the new prisoner. She was surprised to find that the prostitute was a eunuch wearing a yellow-coloured micro-mini! All the women were flustered and worried about their privacy because the new inmate was not the same gender as they were. Usha Maa raised this concern with the superintendent, but there was no immediate clarity in the manuals or procedures for handling such instances. Usha Maa suggested that the new inmate be kept in solitary confinement, and the superintendent agreed. Usha Maa then imitated the eunuch's gait and walked around the barrack. She exaggerated the walk to make all of us laugh. Moments like these made me forget my incarceration, even if for a split second.

Usha Maa also remembered interacting with Yakub Memon's wife, who, according to her, was a beautiful woman who spent all her time praying. She was full of such stories, and would spend whole afternoons regaling us with them sometimes. Having spent twelve years in Yerwada Jail, she had also gained a good understanding of the law. She would often speak to me in Jaya Chheda's absence. She was close to Jaya Chheda, who had warned her not to speak to me. Usha Maa managed a nice balancing act when it came to me, though she was harsh on the other inmates. Her best advice for me was to keep my focus on prayers and God, and stay out of the murky jail politics.

9

MEETING A
STALWART: JYOTIRMOY DEY

I was utterly confident that the lead I had on Pradeep
Sharma was a page-one story. My sources had confirmed
that Sharma was under the scanner for his role in the
Lakhan Bhaiya encounter. Ramnarayan Gupta, alias
Lakhan Bhaiya, was eliminated by Sharma's team in an
allegedly fake encounter in 2006 that had taken place at
the Nana Nani Park in Versova. This park was supposed
to be a place for senior citizens to enjoy a breath of fresh
air and the shoot-out had disrupted its serenity. The police
commissioner's office at Crawford Market was known as
the 'Compound' in crime-reporting circles, and I often
visited high-ranking officers there. I asked one of the very
senior, decorated officers for a quote on my lead, but he
merely raised an eyebrow in surprise.

'Who told you about this?' he asked.

'My sources from the court,' I said. 'Is the news true?'

He nodded. 'The case is at an early stage. Wait for the right time to break it.'

I decided to hold on to Pradeep Sharma's story for the moment. Fifteen days later, I joined *Mid-Day* with high aspirations. *Mumbai Mirror* was giving *Mid-Day* a run for its money. I was riding a wave of confidence over my performance at *Mumbai Mirror*, where I had contributed a minimum of two front-page stories every week. Meenal, who was known to be a strict taskmaster, did play a role is pushing all the reporters, including me, to dig out the best stories. *Mid-Day*, I thought, would be a cakewalk because according to industry sources, the work pressure was lesser than that at *Mumbai Mirror* and there was no push to deliver page-one scoops.

I began working on a story related to Iqbal Kaskar, who was threatening the residents of a building in his area to empty the premises. Since this story had an underworld link, it again required me to visit the Compound and meet the same high-ranking officer whom I was pursuing for the Pradeep Sharma story. My frequency of visiting the Compound increased. Deepak Lokhande, the bureau chief at *Mid-Day* and my boss, felt that the Iqbal Kaskar story could go into the Sunday edition, which was managed by a separate Sunday team. I filed the Kaskar story, thinking that his association with Dawood Ibrahim would propel the story to page one. But I was deflated to find that the story was published as a feature in the middle pages. On inquiring around the office, I was told that 'story mein masala nahi tha' (there was no spice in the story). Further digging revealed that the story had not pleased the resident editor, Shishir Joshi.

Mid-Day had a culture of multiple bosses. There was no pressure in the newsroom. At Mumbai Mirror, Meenal would fling papers in the air and shake up the entire office at 10 p.m. if page one wasn't up to the mark. That kind of pressure often left even seasoned reporters in tears. At first, I enjoyed the low amount of stress at Mid-Day, but as time passed, it put me in an unwanted comfort zone. I began missing the vibe of Mumbai Mirror.

I would file exclusive stories every day, but Deepak would say they were not 'Mid-Day-type'. But there was no guidance or lead from the Mid-Day editors on what exactly they wanted in the paper. There was no push from Deepak. We had to list our stories weekly, on Monday mornings. Each reporter updated Deepak on the stories they would chase over the next six days. At Mumbai Mirror, we would list stories every day. And there was always a risk of the story being rejected by Meenal at the last moment. By the time the edit meeting at Mumbai Mirror concluded around 6 p.m., only three to four stories remained on the list while the others would be struck off. Mid-Day, on the other hand, used whatever the reporter had to offer. At times, I would internally question their editorial decision on front-page stories. I had started to get an inkling that my stories were not being considered on the front-page spot deliberately.

My equation with Prasad Patil at *Mid-Day* was very cold. He had an experience in court reporting, and I believed that he looked at me as competition. At times, I felt he was responsible for killing my stories. The mere sight of him would make me turn red in anger. During that time, a new reporter with no earlier experience was assigned to cover the high court. I was covering the sessions court as a special correspondent. The new reporter's stories regularly made it to page one, while exclusive and worthy stories filed by me were being dumped inside. Mentally, I blamed it all on Prasad Patil.

Apart from the lack of inspiration, I also disliked some of the people at *Mid-Day*. A senior editor sat in a glass cabin right across my desk. He would often adjust his seat in a manner that allowed him to stare at me. Often, he messaged about how well I was dressed, or how attractive my smile was. His attention made me very uncomfortable.

After a couple of uneventful weeks at *Mid-Day*, I was rostered into the night shift, which began late at night and ended at 7.30 a.m. One morning, I was packing up to leave for home when I saw a man in his forties speaking on the landline phone in the cubicle opposite me. It was unusual for a print reporter to show up so early in the morning. I walked up to a female colleague in the features team who was working the same shift. As she stayed in Mulund, we would travel together. I asked her about the person whispering on the phone so secretively.

'You don't know him?' she said, aghast. 'He is J. Dey.'

'Which department?' I asked.

'He is the investigations editor.'

I recalled hearing J. Dey's name crop up in a conversation with Unnikrishnan at *Mumbai Mirror*. While I was working there, Unni was reading the *Hindustan Times* in the corridor with another colleague. They were speaking in Malayalam and happened to mention my name. I had asked Unni what the conversation was about. He mentioned appreciatively that my story had been followed by J. Dey, who was then a crime reporter with *HT*. The story was related to RDX supplies for the 7/11 Mumbai train blasts. But I hadn't noticed J. Dey's stories on the front page of *Mid-Day*. I blamed it on my lack of interest in reading the newspaper as none of my stories were being taken seriously. While I was with *Mumbai Mirror*, I would grab a copy first thing in the morning to check my stories. I would look at the layout, the edit, the photographs, and feel my heart swell with pride. My move to *Mid-Day* now felt like career suicide.

A few days later, in the complex of the *Mid-Day* office, I saw J. Dey leaning against a car and smoking with Iqbal Mamdani, who was a reporter with India TV. Iqbal knew me well and called me over. He asked questions about life at *Mid-Day*, to which I only had half-hearted responses. He expressed surprise that my stories were not showing up on the front page any more, and that made me all the more worried. Iqbal did not introduce me to J. Dey and neither did J. Dey speak to me on his own. Throughout my journalistic career, I had never been introduced to J. Dey, despite him being a renowned crime reporter. Our interactions were simply limited to acknowledging each other's presence with glances and nothing more.

Around four months after joining *Mid-Day*, I received a call from the senior officer from the Compound. He confirmed that the time was ripe to break the Pradeep Sharma story. I filed a story without mentioning Sharma's name. The story read that a decorated encounter specialist was about to be arrested in a fake encounter case. I was excited that I was finally going to get a byline of *Mid-Day*'s front page. But to my shock, the story was confined to a single column at the bottom of page number four. That day, I barged into editor Shishir Joshi's cabin.

'What on earth is this?' I said. 'This story was page-one material!'

Shishir uncrossed his legs and looked up from his laptop. 'Why do you think so, Jigna?'

'This policeman is the most feared encounter specialist in Mumbai Police.'

'But you haven't named him in the report.'

'He hasn't been arrested yet. How can I name him?'

'That is exactly why the story is not on page one,' he said in a calm tone.

I turned around in a huff and left, pretty sure that the story would have been a page-one story at *Mumbai Mirror* or any other newspaper for that matter. A few days later, I received an unexpected call from Hussain Zaidi. He inquired about the story on Pradeep Sharma. I nonchalantly replied that it was a story that came my way, and I had pursued it. He realized I had no idea of the feathers I had ruffled, and hung up.

In the six months that I worked with *Mid-Day*, I had only one page-one story. It was a sting operation involving a public prosecutor from Mazgaon accepting bribe. I felt lifeless at *Mid-Day*. The reporter inside me was in a state of turmoil. I had witnessed the dull office come to life only once during my stint. It was the day when Benazir Bhutto was assassinated on 27 December 2007. I was asked to get a quote from a famous lawyer, which I dutifully did. That day, reporters weren't allowed to leave until the edition was sent to print. But some of the editors did not even leave the comfort of their cabins.

Perhaps the best part of working with *Mid-Day* was the food in the canteen.

I started looking out for newer opportunities. During those days, there were murmurs about *Deccan Chronicle* taking over the *Asian Age* and that they were sprucing up the reporting team. Hussain Zaidi was the resident editor at *Asian Age*. In March 2008, I called him and asked if he was looking to hire a court reporter. I was not sure if he would consider me for the vacancy. To my surprise and relief, he asked me to come over for an interview.

10

THE OUTSIDERS

The day I was remanded to judicial custody and sent to Byculla Jail, my lawyer asked me to contact Elizabeth, a Nigerian inmate, in case I needed any help. He had said it without any further explanation, but I knew he meant I had to go to her in case I was harassed too much in prison. Fortunately, the fact that the inmates and cops both knew I was a journalist helped, and I was saved from any major harassment. They believed I had influential contacts, and never crossed my line. So, I didn't go out searching for Elizabeth.

Barrack No. 2, where I was lodged, had no Africans. They were all housed in Barracks 3, 4 and 5 on the first floor. A few days later in mid-December, during a routine visit to Dr Khan, the jail doctor, I inadvertently ran into Elizabeth. She was a young woman, about twenty-four years old, with curly hair. I was surprised to find out that she could speak in fluent Hindi and Marathi.

After some perfunctory conversation, she herself told me why she was in jail.

'They arrested me at Mumbai airport,' she said in Hindi. 'I was carrying drugs.'

'How long ago was that?'

'Six years, almost,' she said.

'And how did you learn to speak Hindi?'

'Oh, there's a story behind it,' she said.

Apparently, the police officials at the Mumbai airport had detected tiny pouches of drugs that she had swallowed. This was her first trip to India as a drug mule. After her arrest, she had been brought to Byculla Jail. For most inmates, a court hearing is scheduled every fourteen days, but foreigners like Elizabeth often have no lawyers. She also did not receive any support from her embassy and her first court visit was scheduled only three months after her arrest. This too was made possible because of the fellow Africans lodged in the jail who had helped her get a lawyer. Once she settled down in the prison, some of the fellow inmates whom she had befriended promised to teach her Hindi. She was told that if she could communicate in the language with the judge, she might be released early. Elizabeth was a fast learner. Her Hindi training went on for days.

On the day of the hearing, Elizabeth was taken to the court, and when the judge called out her name, she folded her hands and bowed in an elaborate 'namaste', just like she had been taught. The judge appeared pleased, and he smiled and asked her another question. In response, Elizabeth parroted the next line that was taught to her.

'*Teri maa ki chut.*'

Before the horrified judge could speak, Elizabeth dropped the next shocker.

'*Teri maa ka bhosda,*' she shouted.

The people seated in the court burst out laughing. The judge yelled for the police to drag Elizabeth out of his court. She didn't even realize what she had done wrong, and only kept repeating what she was taught. On the way back to jail, in the police van, a woman constable explained to Elizabeth what she had said and the consequences of her actions. On returning to Byculla Jail, Elizabeth got into a fight with the inmates who had played this joke on her. After that, Elizabeth did not get a court hearing for six months. But that made her determined to closely observe and learn the local language. And her effort showed clearly. I had lived in Mumbai most of my life, but Elizabeth's Marathi could put mine to shame.

The Africans were the strongest close-knit group in the jail. The other inmates had branded all Africans as Nigerians. But these women were from various countries of the African continent, some that I had never even heard of. Born in poverty, most of these women had got on the wrong side of the law for small amounts of money. Many of them had HIV, because of which some inmates stayed away from them. Almost all the inmates would suffix their name with the word 'mumma' while addressing them, especially the elder women, to show respect.

Over the course of my term, I befriended a lady called Melody Mumma who had been incarcerated for ten years. She was in her fifties, tall and thin, and a motherly figure for the others in her group. She and her boyfriend had boarded separate flights to Mumbai and Delhi respectively. Both of them were carrying drugs that were a part of a consignment that Melody's son-in-law was shipping to India. And both of them were arrested. Melody was sent to Byculla Jail, and her boyfriend was sent to Tihar Jail.

'There's a lot of poverty back home,' Melody Mumma said. 'So, I agreed to carry drugs to India for 500 dollars.'

'You risked a jail term for such a low amount?'

'In my country 500 dollars is a lot of money actually,' she said. 'We are so poor that some girls don't get food to eat, and they have to solicit customers for as little as two or three dollars.'

That explained why most of these women had HIV. They were forced into prostitution to feed themselves and their families. And since they were not educated about the use of protection or safe sexual practices, they ended up contracting this deadly disease. The irony was that they were unaware of their condition until they landed up in Byculla Jail, where a blood test was carried out mandatorily. This is when most of them were told that they had HIV. The inmates infected with HIV received free medical treatment and support from various NGOs who worked with the jail authorities. Melody Mumma confessed that they would get no medical treatment in their own countries.

'Jail is better than home,' she said. 'We get three meals a day here. And this place is more hygienic.'

But that did not stop her from praying for her release. Her boyfriend had managed to secure bail from Tihar, and he was trying to get bail for her. She often read from a book called *Prayer Rain*, by Dr D.K. Olukoya, which she claimed was the most powerful and practical prayer manual ever written. Melody Mumma would often wake up at 3 a.m. and whisper prayers while reading from the book.

'If you read this book,' she said, 'you will get bail soon. You are a good soul.'

Melody Mumma also gave me a copy of the Bible. The thing with jail is that it makes you cling to the smallest glimmer of hope you can find. I had never fasted all my life, but in Byculla Jail I began fasting to please the gods, in the hope that I would be set free. I also started observing *maun vrat*s (silence). In those periods of silence, I would not speak a word to others around me. And I started reading from *Prayer Rain*. These little trysts with spirituality gave me the strength to tide over the difficult times. When I left prison, I purchased a copy of *Prayer Rain*, and continued reading from it on the nights I could not sleep at home. A year after I was released, Melody was convicted for carrying drugs. But since she had already spent more time in jail than what her sentence provided for, she was set free.

Usha Maa, the warden, had told me that the Africans were extremely difficult to control during the first few days of their term.

'Why?' I asked.

'They are all drugs addicts,' she said. 'The withdrawal makes them agitated.'

'How did you restrain them, then?'

'The severe cases are sent for rehabilitation at J.J. Hospital.'

*

I wasn't used to taking naps in the afternoon, but I would feel so lethargic in jail that I would sleep for three hours every afternoon. At nights, when the inmates would gather to watch 'Voice of India' on TV, a song-based reality show, I would doze off right in the middle of the programme. At times, I thought that my mind and body had adopted sleep as an escape. But the inmates told me another story. In order to maintain order, the jail food was laced with sedatives, they said.

When I was reporting, gangster Abu Salem and terrorist Ajmal Kasab had made similar allegations about the jail food. At that time, I had laughed it off, thinking that the criminals were trying to simply create a fuss. But now, I had doubts.

During a visit to Dr Khan, I asked him if my fears about the food were true. He vehemently denied it. But Usha

Maa seemed to agree with the rumours of the sedatives. 'They lace the food with some chemicals to put off sexual desire,' she said. 'Else the entire jail will be full of lesbian activity.'

Usha Maa advised me against talking to an African inmate called Yusuf Mumma, who was said to be in a lesbian relationship with another inmate. Inmates having sex with each other wasn't uncommon in Byculla Jail at all.

The African inmates would be very happy when any inmate would walk out of the Byculla Jail after acquittal or bail. This was unlike the local inmates, who only reserved jealously for each other. The locals would hurl the choicest of curses on those who were about to get their freedom back. The Africans never complained about the quality of food. Since they could not bear the spice of Indian cuisine, their food was prepared separately, and though it was as bad as what was served to the rest of us, it was still better than what they could eat back home. They also actively participated in the Holi celebrations conducted by Pragya Singh Thakur. They were a lively group who stood with each other through thick and thin. For Christmas, they procured grapes and managed to ferment it into wine, which was given in small quantities to all inmates. We sipped on the wine while the Africans sang *'Jingle Bells'* and other carols. On New Year's Eve, the Africans would throw a sort of a party after taking due permission from the authorities. They would sing songs and dance the night away. I was amazed at the sight of this celebration in jail. But these gatherings served as a good distraction.

The Africans would plan their hospital visits in advance. Going to J.J. Hospital was a chance for the African women to meet their male counterparts from Arthur Road Jail, who would arrange a visit at the same time. Once, I arranged for a check-up at J.J. and sent word to my sister-in-law and my son Nishil to meet me at the hospital. As the police van drove me to the hospital, I passed by the famous Almas Restaurant. I loved the food, and it was my place of choice to catch up with my sources when I was a journalist. The mere sight of the hotel made me hungry. When I reached the hospital, Nishil was already waiting with a packet of chicken biryani from Almas. I was touched by his gesture, but I had given up on non-vegetarian food in the hope of securing an early release. Though I did not eat the food, I hugged him for the care he had shown. I put on a strong face for him. If he saw me crying, he would feel all the more miserable. We spoke a lot for two hours, until the cops came. Then it was time to go back to the barracks again.

Once a month, the court magistrate would visit the jail for an inspection. On these days, the quality of the food would be extremely good so that no inmate could complain about it. The jailer would often make it a point to introduce me to the magistrate. But for me, the introduction would always be an embarrassment, given the fact that I was a journalist who was now in prison. I would look at the floor, and answer the magistrate's questions in monosyllables, unable to meet his eye. I dreaded being introduced to the magistrates so much that I would pray for a court visit to be scheduled whenever their inspection was due.

*

One day, after the bandi, a constable came up to my barrack. 'Jigna,' she said. 'IG sahab has called you to his office.'

I wondered why the inspector general of prisons wanted to see me in his cabin at such a late hour. All sorts of worrying thoughts flooded my mind. Had the Crime Branch officials cooked up more evidence against me? Was my family okay? As the constable led me towards the IG's cabin, Pushpa Kadam, the jailer, came around with a worried look.

'What did you do this time?' she asked.

'Nothing,' I said.

'Did you complain against us in the court?'

I shrugged. 'No.'

The walk to the IG's office would have hardly been two minutes from the barrack, but it felt like an hour. Outside the cabin, the constable ordered me to take off my footwear and enter the cabin. I did as I was told, and nervously stepped inside. I was surprised to see Surinder Kumar, the inspector general (prisons), standing up to greet me. He was wearing a chequered blue shirt.

In 2009, while working for the *Asian Age*, I was part of a media delegation that had accompanied the additional chief secretary (home) to Gadchiroli, a Naxal-affected area in the interiors of Maharashtra. Since this was a conflict zone, the additional chief secretary was provided with Z+ security. Kumar was then posted as the IG of the Gadchiroli range, and he was entrusted with the security of the media delegation, which included four reporters from various publications, including me. After we landed at Nagpur airport, Kumar had personally accompanied me in his official Ambassador car to the village, where we were briefed about various development initiatives taken by the government. A rehabilitation centre for naxals was inaugurated. During our interaction, I had found him to be an extremely courteous officer.

And now I was standing before Kumar as an accused in a murder case. As he stood up from his desk, his eyes fell on my bare feet. Immediately, he pressed a bell and called for the constable who was standing outside his office. He asked her why I was not wearing any footwear. When the constable cited the norm, he advised her to ensure it did not happen to me again. Then I put my sandals back on. Strangely, it felt like a bit of my dignity had been restored. He asked me to take a seat.

'How did you land up here, Jigna?' he said.

'I don't know, sir,' I said. 'I haven't committed any crime.'

'Yes,' he said. 'I am sure there is some misunderstanding. The system has a way of targeting upright people.'

He went on to explain how he had never bowed down to political pressure, and to the lure of easy money, during all his years of service. For that reason, he had often been sidelined from good postings, and he found himself in obscure positions, like this one, that did no justice to his abilities. Even then, he was trying to make a difference with his initiatives.

'You have been here for a month and a half,' he said. 'How can we make things better for the inmates?'

'Sir, the food is really terrible,' I said. 'The rotis are inedible. Even if some of us are on the wrong side of the law, we are still humans and our basic need for food must be protected.'

He took notes in his diary. 'Okay,' he said. 'I will have a copy of the jail manual sent to you. Please read it and let me know what other reforms are needed.'

He stood up again and shook my hand, and also advised me to keep faith in the judiciary. His words lifted my sagging morale, and I was thankful for the respect he had shown to me. Back in the barrack, around 7 p.m., the constable provided me with the jail manual. The next morning, the entire jail was abuzz with news of my meeting with the IG. Many inmates lined up to ask me questions. Some wanted to know if I could ask for favours, some were curious if I was going to be set free. Some were just more friendly to me because of my newly visible connections and some prodded me about what the IG and I had talked about. The topic was discussed for several days and I could feel that the inmates assumed that I had a certain hold. But the attention I had grabbed had not gone down well with Jaya Chheda, who feared losing her hold over the jail.

THE OUTLIERS

11

THE RISE AND FALL

Deccan Chronicle was a revered brand in south India. The *Asian Age* was a publication part of the group, and it commanded great respect too. I was told that A.T. Jayanthi, the senior-most editor of *Asian Age*, would interview me before a final call on my hiring was taken. In March 2018, while the city enjoyed Rang Panchami, I sat at the office in Todi Industrial Estate, Lower Parel, waiting to be called in. The exterior of the office was like a garage shed. Strangely, a long car covered with a plastic sheet that had gathered a thick layer of dust remained parked in the compound. It was only later that I learnt it was a high-end silver-coloured Mercedes.

The exterior of the office was not impressive, but the newsroom inside had a fresh decor and a cosy vibe, with yellow bulbs that gave it a non-corporate feel. Hussain Zaidi led me to Jayanthi's cabin. I was surprised to see her. She had an uncanny resemblance to my ex-boss, Meenal.

'She is Jigna Vora. She has covered some fantastic stories. But these days, I don't see her name on the front pages.'

'Hussain wants you on board,' Jayanthi said. 'What can you bring to the *Asian Age*?'

'I am good at court reporting,' I said. 'And I also have some experience with crime reporting.'

'Full-fledged operations begin in a month,' Hussain said. 'Can you join by then?'

The *Asian Age* had just been taken over by *Deccan Chronicle*, and they were hiring a whole new team, right from resident editor to reporter. Though the paper was in circulation, a lot was going to change.

I agreed. I negotiated for a decent salary package and a higher designation too. It was a smooth interview. I couldn't be happier. I joined the *Asian Age* in May 2008. It was not exactly a pleasant first day as I walked in and was welcomed by a smiling Prasad Patil. He too had quit *Mid-Day* and joined the *Asian Age* as a political reporter. My apprehensions about him were allayed by Zaidi sir who told me not to worry as I would be reporting directly to him, not Patil. I started story-hunting very enthusiastically again. Among the first stories I broke was matka king Suresh Bhagat's fear of threat to his life, which the police had ignored. My story, along with the picture of Jaya Chheda and Suhas Roge in a pool, sent ripples in the fraternity.

Abu Salem was still making news in 2008. I had some information about the love letters that actress Monica Bedi had written to him while both of them were in jail. I knew it would make for a great story, and pursued the lead diligently. Eventually, I found a way to the source who was in possession of those letters. I finally met him while he was shopping for the body-hugging T-shirts that Salem wore to court hearings. After much chasing, I obtained the letters. No one else in the media had a whiff of this. I was excited. A great story always gave me a rush.

The letters were romantic, sexual and desperate. Some even had explicit drawings made by Monica. She sounded like a lover anxiously longing for her partner. But to print the story, Hussain Zaidi asked me to get a quote from Monica Bedi herself.

Monica had already been released from Hyderabad jail. She was going to appear in the second season of the popular reality show *Bigg Boss*, and was seeking interactions with the media through her public relations (PR) team. I got in touch with her PR agency to arrange an interview, but I hid my real objective, which was to get her quote on her love letters to Salem. As arranged, I waited for Monica outside a mall in Thane. She arrived in a car, and I sat in between her and another woman, whom Monica never introduced to me. A bouncer was sitting on the front seat, next to the driver. The car began to move towards Andheri from Ghodbunder Road. After a few lines about her Bollywood comeback, I asked Monica if she had written any love letters to Salem from jail. Instantly, the colour drained from her decked-up face. She was stunned.

'I have those letters,' I said. 'I need a quote from you for the story.'

She insisted that I should not publish her letters. I told her it wasn't my decision but my editor's. She asked her driver to stop, and the car screeched to a halt.

'Get out of my car,' she said.

I exited without being told again and took a taxi to the office. Eventually, the story was printed. The story was sensational and made it to the front page of the *Asian Age*. It created quite a storm. The TV media wanted a copy of the letters to follow up. Aariz Chandra, a TV reporter, requested a copy from me. I consulted Hussain Zaidi and he advised me against sharing the letters with anyone. He was working on a book on Abu Salem, and the letters would provide meaty details for it. At times, I have wondered if my professional equation with Aariz took a hit because of this. He stopped talking to me after that day.

Years later, sitting in Byculla Jail, I realized that Salem himself wanted those letters to come out in the media. This was his revenge against Monica for ditching him. A journalist may think he or she is breaking a story, but the journalist is seldom aware of the hidden agenda behind it. Journalists are often used by cops, politicians, gangsters and film stars to propagate their agenda.

*

In 2008, I covered the Ahmedabad blasts for the *Asian Age*. Rakesh Maria arrested a bunch of Indian Mujahideen operatives after an email claiming responsibility for the blast was traced to Navi Mumbai. From my sources in Ahmedabad, I obtained a photograph of Mansoor Asghar Peerbhoy, who was an accused in the case. And then, from Mumbai, I managed to get a copy of his signature. The signature was sent for handwriting analysis to an expert, without revealing the identity of the person in question. The report confirmed that the handwriting belonged to a terrorist. Once the story was printed, it spread like wildfire and the entire media latched on to it. It was another feather in my cap.

After the 26/11 terror attacks, in December 2008, Hussain Zaidi got an offer to work as a consultant on a documentary on the 26/11 attacks with Channel Four. I was helping him with the research and interviews. For this documentary, we were chasing some video footage of terrorist Ajmal Kasab's interrogation by the police. My source called me to Andheri, late one night. I took along a friend, Murtuza Dewan, and drove with him at the late hour. The source seemed to have risked a lot to get me the CD.

'Call for help if I don't return in fifteen minutes,' I told Murtuza.

I walked into an office where I met my source and two unknown men. As soon as I got the CD, I rushed back, and Murtuza drove us back. We managed to reach the

Asian Age office safely. I was overwhelmed by what I had managed to get. That footage of the terrorists is the only one that is out till date, and was sourced by me. Hussain Zaidi commended me for a good job. The video was used in the documentary as well. Till date, nobody knows who leaked the CD. The source who had passed on the CD to me was only a middleman.

In May 2010, Himanshu Roy took over as joint commissioner, law and order. I had met him earlier when he was additional commissioner, south region, at his office in Nagpada. The meeting was not for journalistic pursuits, but I had been egged on to meet him by many female colleagues who couldn't stop blushing about his personality, muscular physique and sophisticated manner. I went to see him, using a lame excuse for a story, and handed my visiting card to his assistant. I was called into his cabin. The moment I entered his room he cast a glance at my biscuit-coloured skirt and white shirt. He immediately stood up and pulled out a chair for me with the flourish of a gentleman.

'Can I get some tea for you?' he asked in his smooth voice.

I politely declined and spoke to him briefly about an irrelevant case from Colaba. I walked out of his office thoroughly impressed. Then, giggling like a teenager, elated to meet such a polished man, I met Hussain Zaidi at office. Hussain Zaidi warned me to be careful about my appearance when I went for professional meetings, and not be too friendly. His words turned out to be prophetic later.

As I started reporting more on crime, the frequency of my meetings with Himanshu increased. I would often hear rumours about my affair with him, but I laughed them off. It did feel strange when junior police officers began requesting me to push for better postings with Himanshu. Male reporters from the fraternity played their part in spreading these rumours. They would be waiting for long hours outside Himanshu's cabin for a quote, and I would be called in before them. They would be oblivious to the fact that I would take an appointment from Himanshu's office days in advance and show up on time.

It did not help that Himanshu addressed me with quite a few adjectives in private conversations. He would often call me 'sweetheart', etc. I would always address him as 'sir'. Truth be told, Himanshu never gave me even one big story in all that time. In fact, he always discouraged me from pursuing certain leads. On one rainy evening, I was sitting inside Himanshu's cabin for a quote on the deportation of gangster Santosh Shetty. He was sitting with his hands behind his head, in a blue chequered half-sleeved shirt. The white T-shirt he wore inside was visible at the seams. He looked directly into my eyes and flexed his biceps suggestively.

'Sir!' I said firmly. 'Your muscles don't excite me.'

His biceps stopped flexing, and I realized that I had perhaps crossed a line, but it was important that I made my stance clear to him. Though he had never made a direct pass at me, his demeanour indicated that it was leading towards it. I wanted to stop things before they went any further.

A few days later, in late December 2010, I received a tip-off about a well-known builder who was into shady land dealings, and his exchanges with Himanshu. Like a fool, I asked Himanshu if this was true, even though I wasn't doing a story on it. Himanshu brushed off the allegation, but this kind of rash behaviour on my part ended up ruffling a lot of feathers with powerful people. Later, I confronted many senior police officials about this information. A certain hubris had taken over me. Perhaps, this played a part in my downfall.

*

In December 2010, once, I attended a press conference (PC) at the Crime Branch and sat in the last row. After the PC, I met Himanshu for a quote on an exclusive story. A man whom I had met from a matrimonial site happened to call at that time. Usually, I didn't answer calls when meeting police officials, but I answered the phone that day to let him know that I would call him after my meeting with the JCP (Crime) came to an end.

'Boyfriend?' Himanshu asked as soon as I had hung up.

'Hmmm.'

'Strange that you would want to marry someone you met online,' he said.

I was surprised. 'So what?' I said, defiantly.

His eyes became big and red. For a moment I was scared. How did he know that the man I was contemplating to marry was someone I had met online? Had he tapped my phone? I decided to be more careful in my interactions with Himanshu from then on.

On 8 June 2011, I visited Himanshu's office for a quote on another story. I was scheduled to fly to Sikkim the next day. Himanshu mentioned how things were calm in the city. I casually joked that this was the proverbial lull before a storm. He laughed at that and wished me a safe journey. Three days later, J. Dey was shot dead.

12

JAIL'S MANDAKINI

One night in Byculla Jail, I woke up to the clanging of heavy anklets. A sight awaited my weary eyes. Fifty-year-old Salma Bibi was prancing around the barrack, clad in nothing but a thin, red dupatta that was draped around her torso, tied in a peculiar knot above her cleavage. Her saggy breasts drooped down to her paunch. With each heavy movement, her big hips swayed from one side to the other. The silvery anklets were shining around her dark legs.

Earlier in the day, she had passed me in the reception area, wearing a cream-coloured salwar-kameez and hurling the kind of abuses I hadn't ever heard before. Hence, I maintained my silence as she went about her naked antics that night, running her hands through her shoulder-length, salt-and-pepper hair. None of the other inmates seemed perturbed. A lady police constable was standing guard outside the barrack. Salma Bibi walked up to the gates and held the iron bars.

'Why is the court delaying my case?' Salma asked the constable.

The constable looked at Salma and said nothing.

'What are you staring at?' Salma said. 'I'll blow your bloody *choot* off.'

The constable was visibly angry, but she maintained her calm and allowed the abuse to die down, preferring not to escalate the conflict because Salma Bibi's *gaali*s could make one's ears bleed. I knew that most of her frustration stemmed from the slow progress of her case.

Salma had landed up in Barrack No. 2 on account of the various ailments she was suffering from. Her vision was blurry and she was acutely diabetic. Her designated place was right opposite mine. Each inmate, except the powerful ones, had personal space only as wide as a tile. All of us would sleep around the boundaries of the barrack. No inmate was allowed to sleep in the middle. For dinner, Salma Bibi would sit with her back against the stone walls, wearing only that red dupatta, and extend her legs out, while the aluminium plate would rest on her lap. That sight would kill my appetite, or whatever remained of it.

I learnt more about Salma Bibi when we started talking. She had been in jail for the past one-and-a-half years. Before her arrest, she had lived with her son and second husband in the slums of Ganesh Nagar in Malad.

The family stayed in a ground-plus-one *kholi*, which was a room in a hutment. Her husband was in his mid-sixties and worked as a tailor. It was alleged that Salma Bibi and her son had killed him for the property. On the night that her husband was found dead, Salma Bibi claimed that her son was not even home. She came down the ladder from the first floor to find him dead already. She raised an alarm and alerted the neighbours. The neighbours called the police, who found that the man had an injury on his head. In their statements to the police, the neighbours alleged that the family had been fighting a lot over the property. Now, the police had a motive for the murder. But they didn't recover the weapon. 'If I indeed killed my husband, where is the weapon I used?' Salma Bibi would ask in her defence. She alleged that her husband had most likely fallen on the floor and died accidentally.

The police charged her with the destruction of evidence. Her son was also arrested and sent to Thane Jail. He was married and had a child. Salma claimed her son's family stayed in their native village, but no one knew if that was the truth.

Salma Bibi was originally from Kolkata. After her first husband had died, nearly 25 years ago, she had moved to Mumbai with her son. But she still believed she was the queen of Bengal, and demanded fish curry for dinner every night. There were quite a few Bengali-speaking inmates in Barrack No. 2, and she got along well with some of them, especially Paromita, who often had love bites on her neck.

The inmates suspected these were a result of her dalliances with one of the lady police constables.

Many people warned me against talking to Salma, because she was always ready for a fight. She was in the good books of Jaya Chheda and thus would often receive new clothes and jewellery to wear. Jaya would also arrange packets of biryani for Salma whenever she would visit J.J. Hospital for medical check-ups. Salma would dress up in her best attire for hospital visits, and sing praises of Jaya after she returned. 'Jaya Maa arranged for the best fried fish I have ever tasted!' she would say.

Salma took great pleasure in dressing up for the weekly visit of the male superintendent, whom she lovingly referred to as *Daroga Babu*. On Fridays, when the Daroga Babu would come for the weekly visit, she would drape her favourite white saree, and line her eyes with kajal. She would pin up her *pallu*, and put a red bindi on her forehead. Then, she would hook heavy earrings in her earlobes, and twirl around for a round of praise from the other inmates. Fatima, who had a habit of cracking jokes with sexual overtones, would remark that the superintendent would be floored by the magic of Salma Bibi. Salma would blush like a teenage girl on hearing that, and all the women would burst out laughing!

Each Friday, when the superintendent would arrive at 9.30 a.m., Salma would stand as close as she could get to him. The superintendent would ask the inmates if there was anything he could do for their betterment, and Salma would get in his face and point to her left eye, which would flicker continually due to her blurry vision.

'Daroga Babu,' she would say, *'meri aankh ka toh kuch karo.'*

The superintendent would move a step back. *'Haan, haan. Karta hoon.'*

She would move forward a step. *'Kab karoge? Jaldi karo.'*

All the women would chuckle, and the superintendent would exit hastily.

Salma Bibi also had a huge problem with the amount of money the Indian government had spent on the security of Ajmal Kasab, the only terrorist who was caught alive for his role in the 26/11 terror attack. 'These *madarchod*s spent four-and-a-half crore to keep that terrorist alive!' she would say. 'But nobody cares that I am going blind.'

She would often notice me poring over a newspaper from the far end of the barrack and guess which article I was reading. 'How come you were able to see what I was reading?' I would ask her.

'Utna toh dikhta hai,' she would reply.

Salma would often wake up in the middle of the night and hurl mindless abuses. Sometimes, she would sit alone in the veranda and talk to herself. Once, I sat next to her in a moment of solitude. After a while she turned to me and said, 'I'll go back to Bengal after my acquittal. I don't like Mumbai any more.'

Salma Bibi had an undying belief that she would be set free in due course of time. Jaya Chheda had promised Salma that she would use all her influence to get her released. Salma clung to that belief as if her life depended on it.

'I committed no crime,' she would tell me. 'Why should I be afraid of any court?'

For such small favours, Jaya used Salma like her personal servant in jail. I learnt that Salma's son was also playing a similar role for Jaya's son in Thane Jail. Jaya often used to give freebies to inmates. After Jaya came back from hospital in February, she gave Salma a pair of nighties to wear. After that, Salma gave up draping the thin dupatta over her naked body. I noticed that Jaya had built an army of personal assistants with her influence. Most of these were Africans and inmates accused of murder. Jaya had convinced some of those accused of murder that it was impossible for them to get bail, so that they could stay in jail and serve her.

Paddu, who was Paromita's helper, once told me that she would never get bail.

'Why?' I asked.

'Jaya Maa has said so,' Paddu said.

I asked for Paddu's charge sheet, and read it. I told her that she had been taken for a ride because bail was possible in her case. She didn't even have a lawyer. Many of the accused do not have the money or resources to arrange lawyers to fight their cases. And the NGOs who work in Byculla Jail also prefer helping only those inmates who can pay them. I had seen an NGO representative asking an inmate for Rs 500 to deliver a message to her home. The ones who do not have money are neglected and left to their fate. I managed to arrange a lawyer, Raja Thakur, for Paddu.

One day, Salma returned to the barracks after a court visit, heartbroken. She walked around the barracks like a hurt animal, hurling every abuse she knew in Bengali. I couldn't understand much of it, but no one had ever seen her so disturbed. I didn't even have the courage to console her because Jaya was keeping a constant watch on my activities, either personally or through her informers. Finally, Paromita walked up to Salma, and spoke to her in Bengali. They had an animated conversation, and I heard Jaya's name pop up a few times. At that time, Jaya was visiting court because her trials had a daily hearing, so perhaps Salma was less discreet than she would have normally been.

Later, Paromita told me what had transpired. The Dindoshi court was hearing Salma's case, and Jaya had promised to arrange the best lawyer for her. The lawyer in question was none other than the famous Mahesh Patil, who was the go-to person for any case in Dindoshi. During one of her court visits, Salma ran into Mahesh Patil and asked him why he wasn't showing up for her case. The seasoned lawyer blew the lid off Jaya's lies. He said he had never been paid to argue for Salma's case and had no reason to show up.

'Jaya has fucked up Salma's case,' Paromita said.

'What do we do now?' I asked.

'Wait and watch,' she said. 'Keep reading your *Hanuman Chalisa*.'

Paromita was a shrewd woman. Though she sympathized with Salma, a conflict with Jaya would make her survival, or even anyone else's survival, impossible. Her fears proved right because no sooner had Jaya arrived back in her fiefdom, one of her many spies updated her on what had occurred in her absence. Later that night, Salma Bibi applied cold cream all over her body like she did each night, and went to sleep while keeping a fair distance from everyone because even the slightest of unwarranted touches irritated her no end.

In the middle of the night, the entire barrack woke up to loud abuses. Salma Bibi and Simran, the mobile thief, were pulling each other's hair.

'Why did you kick me?' Salma screamed.

'I never touched you, whore!' Simran shouted.

Salma Bibi spat on the floor. 'One *lauda* will never suffice a cocksucker like you!'

They threw wild punches and dragged each other around. The entire barrack watched in stunned silence, and no one had the guts to intervene. Paromita was sure Simran had been egged on by Jaya. The fight got so serious that the jail authorities had to open the locks of the barrack at 2 a.m. Opening the barrack while the bandi was in force was serious. It had never happened in front of me. When they were finally separated, Salma and Simran had clumps of each other's hair in their hands. Immediately, the authorities shifted Salma to a different circle. I didn't get a chance to interact with Salma a lot after that. But I met her once during a visit to Dr Khan.

'Salma Bibi, how is your superintendent?' I asked her in jest.

'He is useless,' she said. 'His lauda can't even stand up.' We all laughed at that.

Salma Bibi had not forgiven Jaya Chheda and wanted her to rot in hell. Her last piece of advice to me was to stay away from Jaya's games, and pray to God for my release.

Much later, I heard about Salma Bibi's death due to tuberculosis. I always remember Salma Bibi as the woman who sat in the veranda of Byculla Jail, and dreamt of living a free life in Kolkata. She always claimed the police had framed her and her son. Sometimes, she was worried about the kholi that had apparently led to her husband's death. She was sure the neighbours would have usurped it by now. Unfortunately, death came to her long before the freedom she longed for. Salma Bibi's son was convicted in the murder case and sentenced to a life term.

13

COLLATERAL DAMAGE

With every passing day, I became more attentive and observant in jail. Some inmates intrigued me, while some made me restless. Suman Soni had the latter effect on me. She had spent about seven months in jail. The forty-something woman was thin to the point of emaciation. She always wore a sari, and her hair would be tied in a neat plait. Her frail arms would show in her loose-sleeved blouses, which she had borrowed from others. Other inmates constantly bullied her, and she did not have the physical or mental strength to stand up for herself. She would speak to no one. Sometimes, I would see her sitting in a corner, talking to herself and crying.

None of Suman's family members ever came to meet her. A long time ago, Suman had also adopted a son, who had turned nineteen while she was in jail, but even he never bothered to check on his foster-mother. Her son's story would force me to confront my own horrid thoughts. What if my son did the same to me? What if he decided to never see me again?

The powerful inmates did minimal cleaning work for the weekly visits of the superintendent. But Usha Maa, the warden, would make Suman scrub the entire barrack, and the poor soul would do it without a murmur of protest. The other inmates would look at her and laugh, as she went about bearing their share of the workload.

I managed to speak to Suman once. The conversation lasted barely thirty minutes. She spoke in chaste Hindi, in an accent that made me guess she was from Uttar Pradesh. Suman had been arrested for attempting to murder her mother-in-law. Married at a young age of twelve, Suman's life was made hell because she could not bear any children. Her mother-in-law tortured her endlessly. Once, she inserted forceps into Suman's vagina and turned them so that her womb could be destroyed forever. I was aghast at the amount of cruelty a woman could unleash on another. As Suman shivered while recalling the tale, I could not stop my tears.

Suman also owned a flat in Jogeshwari area. After her husband died, her mother-in-law insisted that she leave the house and walk away. Her mental and physical torture continued, now for the flat that her mother-in-law wanted. One day, during an argument, Suman snapped. She picked up a wooden plank and hit her mother-in-law on the head. The monstrous lady collapsed on the floor in a pool of blood, but survived, and Suman landed in jail.

The Byculla Jail campus had police quarters right behind our barracks. Every Saturday, around 2 a.m., Suman would start shouting through the small windows that were located at the top of the barrack walls.

'Superintendent sahab!' she would scream. 'You are sleeping so peacefully with your wife. *Mera toh kuch karo!*'

It was her weekly ritual that humoured some inmates but irritated a few others. Salma Bibi would often ask Suman if she wanted the superintendent to 'douse the fire that was burning inside her body'.

I learnt that Suman had no lawyer, and thus no court visits were scheduled for her. She had no clue what a charge sheet meant, and if there was one in her case. I got the address of her Jogeshwari house and requested the NGOs representative visiting the jail to contact someone from her family. But the NGOs took no interest in her case. I pleaded with them to get her a lawyer, but they ignored that request too.

Finally, I spoke to Paromita and we briefly discussed the possibility of getting Suman released. Having studied law, I knew that in Suman's case, bail was possible. Paromita was curious about my interest in helping Suman, and other inmates too began talking about my efforts.

One morning, at around 10 a.m., I found about half a dozen inmates circling Suman, clapping and singing loudly. I walked over to find Suman dressed in a gaudy sari. She had dark red lipstick spread on her lips, a thick outline of kohl around her eyes and dangling earrings.

The inmates forced her to dance and Suman obeyed their orders. More inmates gathered around Suman soon. I shivered as I watched the entire barrack surround her, dancing like a nomadic tribe. Even the Africans danced while Suman remained at the centre. They made it look like Suman was behaving like a eunuch.

Later that day, the jail authorities arrived and took custody of Suman. I wondered why they had taken her away, considering such bullying was not uncommon in the jail. But later on, I learnt that Suman had been transferred to a hospital for mentally disturbed people in Thane. The murmurs began soon after that Jaya Chheda had had a hand in it all and got Suman transferred. My attempts to get Suman bail had not gone down well with Jaya. Before I could do anything, Jaya had played her cards.

*

In April 2012, I read a newspaper report that Mumbai Police had arrested a struggling actress named Simran Sood in relation to the murder of Delhi businessman Arun Tikku. The article and subsequent media coverage created quite a buzz in Byculla Jail. All the inmates were excited about an actress joining their ranks. Vijay Palande was also arrested. Arun Kumar Tikku, sixty-two, had been murdered in his three-bedroom flat in Mumbai by Palande's associates. There was news that Simran would also be charged.

Two weeks later, Simran Sood arrived in Byculla Jail in the evening. She was skinny, tall and fair. She was taken to Barrack No. 2. Inmates from Barrack No. 2 lined up to get a good look at the 'actress'. But to the best of my knowledge, Simran had only been a struggler who had perhaps appeared in a few item songs. Next morning, Simran was shifted to Barrack No. 5. In the afternoon, she came up to speak to me when I was reciting my prayers under the tree, which was my usual place for meditation.

'Can you remove my hair extensions?' Simran asked.

I shook my head. I had never used such accessories and had no clue how to take one off. Simran hadn't been able to remove the extension for the past fifteen days, and now it was pricking her scalp. I suggested that she check with Melody Mumma, since the Africans in jail had short hair and would probably know how to deal with an extension. When Simran visited Melody Mumma, she was finally able to get the extension off her head. She couldn't stop thanking me for the help.

Simran received a lot of attention in jail due to the high-profile nature of her case. She also started spending a lot of time with me. Jaya Chheda could not accept this, and tried her best to cause a rift between us.

Simran was unable to get used to the jail food. Since I had received permission through a court order to be sent home-cooked food, I suggested to Simran that she could try getting one too. Her lawyer tried many times, but the court never allowed Simran the requisite permission.

Simran confided to me that she had been dating a top stockbroker from Mumbai before her arrest. Her lavish lifestyle involved partying and clubbing every single night. She would try designer clothes for hours before finalizing her look each evening, a stark contrast to her life now, when she had only two pairs of clothes. She fondly remembered the new year bash that her stockbroker boyfriend had thrown on a yacht in Goa.

'He booked the entire yacht for me,' she said.

'Did he ever come to meet you when you were in police custody?'

'No,' she said. 'But I'm sure he will visit me here.'

I merely laughed from my own experience and asked her not to expect too much from friends.

'He is a Gujarati,' she said. Then she told me his name, and asked if there was any chance I might be related to him.

'No,' I said.

'Good,' she replied. 'Because his mother is a bitch. A control freak!'

I laughed aloud at that. Simran also mentioned that she used to go shopping to Bangkok every weekend with a coterie of socialites. None of them had bothered to check on her after her arrest. She said she used to also meet Santosh Shetty, Chhota Rajan's associate, in Bangkok. Shetty was extradited to India in 2011. I would often find him sitting in the same vehicles during our court visits.

According to the police, Vijay Palande and Simran were husband and wife, but Simran always insisted that

Vijay was like a brother to her. Other inmates joked about this.

'Oh, yes,' Usha Maa quipped. 'During the day he is your brother, and at night he is your lover!'

I offered some of my kurtas to Simran since she had so few clothes, and we were pretty much the same height. She politely refused because her father was due to visit her from Delhi, where her family lived. While working in Bollywood, Simran had lived alone in Mumbai in a posh locality. Her accent had the forced delicateness of a film star. She would lament about her situation, but I never saw her crying in jail.

Simran was assigned to Barrack No. 5, and her space was next to Melody Mumma. She started reading the Bible, fasting and attending some of the rituals of Muslim inmates on Fridays, all in the hope that there would be some divine intervention that would ensure her release. She also got addicted to the packets of gutkha that Fatima would smuggle inside. To me, Simran often spoke about designer brands of handbags, and I could never even pronounce their names correctly.

Simran had never used an Indian toilet in her life before, but now she was sharing a toilet with forty other women. Earlier, she drank nothing but mineral water, but now she had to drink from dirty taps. Her parties would begin at 12.30 a.m. and end at 5.30 a.m. But in Byculla Jail, she had to wake up at 5.30 a.m. and attend a headcount. The way she spoke about her life, Simran had lived in a way that most of us cannot even dream of.

Simran often joked that once we were released, we would be the perfect candidates for *Bigg Boss*. And she had a plan to go to Goa too. I had never visited Goa before, so I would enthusiastically agree with her. 'We'll have so much fun, it will be once in a lifetime', she would say.

Simran missed her stockbroker boyfriend a lot. During each court visit, she was hopeful that he would turn up to meet her, but each time she would return in the evening with a dejected look on her face. I could relate to this situation completely since so many of the people I had considered my trusted friends had also forsaken me. But Simran still hoped that her lover would turn up to see her the next time. I did not have the heart to burst her bubble of hope. Her brother and father, and her lawyer would often visit her though.

In May, Jaya Chheda started guiding Simran and told her she was ready to help her if Simran stopped talking to me. However, Simran would wait for Jaya Chheda to leave for her court date and rush to my barrack and chat with me. Simran would often go through the book that was delivered to Jaya every day. Jaya would also get clothes from Westside for her. I never had the courage to tell Simran that Jaya used most inmates like dolls, and she would break her favourite toys as soon as she got bored of them. In Simran's case, that happened rather soon. Late one night, Jaya instigated a fight between an African inmate and Simran. The African inmate slapped Simran hard and her cheeks turned red. The entire jail was stunned. To Simran's credit, not even such a hard slap could make her cry. The lady constables arrived and shifted Simran to Circle 2. After that, I would only meet Simran during doctor visits. She confessed that she missed talking to me. I advised her to keep to herself and not get over-friendly with anyone.

Simran secured bail a few months after me. She made a great effort to keep in touch. Once, I took my son to the KFC at Linking Road, Bandra, and he was enjoying his food when someone called my name aloud. I turned around and saw Simran running towards me. She hugged me tightly. 'You supported me during the worst phase of my life,' she said, and started weeping. That was the only time I saw her cry.

14

THE KILLING OF J. DEY

On the rainy afternoon of 11 June 2011, one piece of news spread among the city's journalists. A journalist had been shot in broad daylight. The telephone line at the police control room rang non-stop. Other journalists wanted to know if it was true or just fake news doing the rounds.

Soon, reports confirmed that fifty-six-year-old Jyotirmoy Dey had been shot near his residence in Hiranandani Gardens, Powai. Later, another update confirmed that J. Dey, as he was famously known, was dead.

J. Dey was the investigations editor at *Mid-Day*. At around 2.30 p.m. on the fateful day, he was returning home after meeting his mother Bina at her Amrut Nagar house in Ghatkopar. Minutes before reaching home, Dey had called his wife to inform her that he would reach in the next 10–15 minutes. By 2.45 p.m., when Dey reached the main road leading to Hiranandani Gardens, four men on two bikes opened fire at him. J. Dey, who was on a motorcycle too, collapsed instantly. He was first rushed to a nearby hospital, which was ill-equipped to treat such severe injuries. He had five gunshot entry wounds and four exit wounds on his body. By the time he was taken to the Hiranandani Hospital, he had succumbed to them.

J. Dey's murder sent shock waves in the journalist fraternity across the country. The six-foot-three imposing man had been one of the top crime reporters. Many juniors looked up to him. Even before he was laid to rest, theories about the possible motive behind his killing began to surface.

Some said that it was the powerful oil mafia that he had irked with his exposés. Some cited the story about red sandalwood smuggling that he was working on as a probable reason. J. Dey's probe about a senior cop's close link with Dawood Ibrahim was another theory that floated around, while some believed that perhaps he had rubbed the underworld the wrong way through his reports.

*

With the onset of the monsoon that year, I had finally found the time to visit Sikkim with my family, a trip that we had planned for months. The pristine, lush valleys were a soothing relief. We were in the picturesque town of Pelling on the afternoon of 11 June 2011, when my Blackberry phone began beeping continuously. The screen flashed Hussain Zaidi's name, my editor at the *Asian Age*.

'What, sir?' I said, in jest. 'Can't I enjoy a vacation without thinking about work?'

'J. Dey has been shot dead,' he replied bluntly. 'Confirm it and file a story. Get all the details.'

The news made me gasp. I gazed at my phone wondering how a journalist could be shot dead in a city like Mumbai. The first person I thought of contacting was Himanshu Roy, who was joint commissioner of police (crime) back then. I promptly dialled Roy's number. The siren of a police jeep wailed in the background, as Roy spoke in a voice laced with urgency. He was on his way to Powai, where the murder had taken place. With the confirmation from the top cop, I called Prasad Patil, the then bureau chief at *Asian Age*. He put another reporter to cover the spot story while I tapped into my sources to get deeper. As soon as I reached my room at the lodge we were staying in, I switched on the television. J. Dey's murder was 'Breaking News' on all the channels. I stopped at NDTV and got back to making calls.

To me, J. Dey was a professional acquaintance. He was an extremely private person who spoke only when he wanted to. My interactions with him were limited to a distant smile, only if we happened to glance at each other at press conferences. My mind kept drifting back to the thought that J. Dey's murder was a stark reminder of the perils of our profession. At around 8.30 p.m., I dictated my inputs to a junior reporter from office. The cellular network was weak in the mountains. But the story was filed.

The next morning, we stepped out early as the sun peeked through the beautiful hillocks. A light drizzle fell on the roof of our Toyota Innova as we drove along the narrow roads to see all the sights. A beautiful mist limited our visibility. Even as I looked at the mesmerizing landscape around, my mind pondered over J. Dey's murder. My family, all eight of them, stopped by to enjoy momos for brunch. But I had no appetite.

My phone buzzed continuously, even while we were in the red corridors of a Buddhist monastery. There were several theories that circulated. The strongest one was that he bore the brunt for reporting aggressively on the oil mafia. But there were no concrete leads and it was all mere speculation. I continued to stay in touch with my colleagues and sources over the next few days.

On 18 June, I returned to Mumbai. I wasted no time and went to Roy's office at Crawford Market. The cops, I learnt, were still clueless. They had absolutely no leads. A large group of journalists had protested by organizing a candle march for their fallen colleague. A delegation also met Home Minister R.R. Patil, demanding a CBI probe in the case. Roy was under tremendous pressure to crack it.

'Did he have any personal animosities?' I asked Roy. 'Disputes?'

'Not that we're aware of,' he said.

'Any suspects at this time?'

'We're exploring all angles.'

'Any leads from the CCTV footage?'

'Like what?'

'Perhaps the CCTV footage can reveal if the shooters escaped towards Andheri or Ghatkopar?'

He held his chin in his hands and contained the faint smile between his thick fingers. 'Why should I reveal the course of my investigation?' I understood his need for secrecy and wished him good luck on the case.

Around that time, I also filed a story about J. Dey's unscheduled trip to London in 2011, allegedly to meet Iqbal Memon alias Iqbal Mirchi, a close associate of fugitive gangster Dawood Ibrahim. Mumbai Police also began investigating this trip.

The media had grown restless. We needed some concrete answers on the murder. On 27 June, exactly sixteen days after J. Dey was murdered in cold blood, Mumbai Police announced a press conference. All of us headed to the Police Press Club at Azad Maidan. I sat in the back row, sipping a cup of tea, as Arup Patnaik, the city's police commissioner, announced that they had an important breakthrough. Standing by the commissioner's side was Roy, his biceps bulging in the chequered, half-sleeved shirt he wore.

'We have arrested seven people. Underworld Don Chhota Rajan is behind the killing,' the cop announced.[3]

---

[3] https://www.indiatoday.in/india/photo/mumbai-police-press-conference-on-j-dey-murder-365761-2011-06-27/3
NDTV, 'Chhota Rajan Gang Had Journalist Dey Killed: Police', https://www.ndtv.com/india-news/chhota-rajan-gang-had-journalist-dey-killed-police-459579

'The murder was planned by Rohit Thangapani, alias Satish Kalia, at the behest of Chhota Rajan. Kalia is a known shooter of Rajan's gang and has worked for him earlier too. While three persons were arrested from Mumbai, three were arrested from Rameshwaram in Tamil Nadu, and one from Solapur.'

The revolver, bullets and the mobile phones used in the murder had been recovered. The cops suspected that the trigger was the two articles written by J. Dey about Chhota Rajan's diminishing influence in the underworld. But the police theory had too many loose ends. Nevertheless, the media congratulated the cops, including Senior Inspector Ramesh Mahale, who was known for his immaculate paperwork.

On 1 July 2011, in an explosive interview to NDTV, Chhota Rajan claimed that J. Dey had been colluding with rival gangster Dawood Ibrahim. On his visit to London, Dey had invited Chhota Rajan for an interview, but the don sensed danger and stayed away. Rajan's suspicion was further strengthened when Dey invited him for an interview in the Philippines. J. Dey had thus turned traitor in the books of Chhota Rajan, a renegade threat that *had* to be eliminated. 'Reporters should not cross their limits,' Chhota Rajan said, concluding the interview.

Vinod Asrani, a builder based in Chembur with links to Chhota Rajan, was also arrested by the Crime Branch. He was known to drink with Dey in the bars of central Mumbai. Around the first week of June, he had allegedly helped the sharpshooters identify J. Dey at a bar named 'Uma Palace' in Mulund, the cops claimed. In each arrest, Mumbai Police pressed charges under the stringent MCOCA against all the accused.

15

DOG EAT DOG

The front-page story in a city tabloid announced that
there had been a development in the J. Dey murder case.
The story stated that the police were closely investigating
the role of a female reporter in the murder, but did not
name the suspect or the policemen. Based on information
provided by highly placed sources, the story managed to
create ripples and perhaps also created anticipation that
there would be a fresh arrest.

Another story in a national daily, buried somewhere in
the middle pages, made a similar claim. A female reporter,
under the police scanner, had allegedly provided the
registration number of J. Dey's bike, his residential address
and his office address to Chhota Rajan, the story stated.

I'd been living in a rented apartment in Worli since
September 2010, because it saved a lot of time travelling to
the nearby *Asian Age* office. I was a single parent, and my

job paid for my son's education, and for the various bills that life never stops throwing at you. In an area where real estate costs a bomb, I paid a modest rent of Rs 12,000 per month because the flat was only a small room redeveloped by the Slum Rehabilitation Authority (SRA).

I closely followed every development in the murder. I wondered who this female reporter was. I turned the page over, not realizing that the sheet of paper in my hands was a ticking time bomb, waiting to explode.

Over the coming days, I noticed that my co-workers at *Asian Age* would pause in the middle of animated conversations if I happened to be passing. Calls to my colleagues in other media houses went unanswered and unreturned. It was sometime towards the end of August 2011 that Zaidi sir called me to his cabin.

'Sit,' he said. 'You've done a good job with the J. Dey case.'

I nodded.

'The police suspect the involvement of a female reporter,' he said. 'Any idea who that might be?'

I shrugged.

'Jigna,' he said, 'it could be a rumour, but the needle of suspicion is pointing at you.'

I sank into the chair, shocked. I assured him I had no role to play, which seemed to put him at ease. Maybe these were mere rumours after all, and they'd die their own death. I had nothing to fear because my conscience was clear. But the rumours only got stronger. And wherever I went, I had a constant paranoia of being followed. I'd turn around and find no one, but I could never shake off that fear. The wildest theory on the grapevine alleged that I'd been a party to the murder because of an affair gone wrong with J. Dey. In reality, I didn't even recall ever speaking to him.

At the same time, Leo, my pug whom I loved to death, was growing increasingly distant. We usually shared a close bond, but at that time, he just didn't want to be anywhere near me. My mom later reasoned that perhaps Leo had an intuition that I was going away from home, and this was his way of preparing for it.

The rumour mills were working overtime. My name cropped up more often in the media fraternity, though the identity of the female reporter was never revealed in the newspapers. I discussed the situation with Hussain Zaidi again, and we agreed it would be best to meet Himanshu Roy and clear the air. On 9 September 2011, with rain lashing down from the dark Mumbai sky, I met Zaidi sir at the Palladium Mall in Lower Parel, where he was accepting delivery of his new car. His wife, a devout Hindu, performed an aarti of the car, and with rain pounding heavily against the windscreen, we reached Crawford Market at 8 p.m. While Zaidi sir attended the meeting with Himanshu Roy, I prayed at the nearby Hanuman temple, pleading with the god of strength to help me tide through this crisis.

I noticed the sombre look on Zaidi's face when he returned. His knuckles whitened as he clutched the steering of his brand-new car tightly.

'Himanshu confirmed they are investigating you,' he said.

'Why?' I said as I burst into tears. 'I haven't done anything!'

'He says a lot of people, some in his circles, and some in ours, will be happy to see you behind bars.'

'Who are these people?'

'These are murky waters, Jigna. Nothing is clear. But he assured me that he knows you aren't involved. And he'll make sure justice prevails in the end.'

My breathing eased. 'I am standing between my men and Jigna's arrest,' Roy had assured Zaidi sir. I wish he had recorded that conversation.

A media association suggested that they'd present my case before the home minister, but I did not proceed because I had no guilt to bear. Like Zaidi sir, I believed in Himanshu Roy's words. Looking back, that was the biggest mistake of my life.

*

My family planned another vacation to Nathdwara, Rajasthan, on 25 November, to visit the holy shrine of Srinathji. The rental lease of the SRA flat in Worli has since ended, and I had returned to Ghatkopar to stay with my grandparents and mother. On 31 October, I woke up to my BlackBerry phone vibrating. Megha Prasad, a friend and a fellow journalist, had sent me numerous messages.

Her panic-stricken words asked me to check the *Mumbai Mirror*. I picked up the paper in front of my door with shaking hands. The front-page report claimed that the police had recovered call recordings in which Chhota Rajan had admitted to unidentified people that the lady reporter had instigated the murder of J. Dey. The police also claimed to be in possession of a threatening text message sent by the female reporter to J. Dey. I was shaken as I finished reading the article. It stated that over the next few days, the Crime Branch was going to call in the reporter for questioning.

In the first week of November, I called Senior Inspector Ramesh Mahale of the Mumbai Crime Branch. He was a deeply religious person.

'God will help you if you're innocent,' he said.

'I haven't done anything, sir.'

'Good,' he said. 'Then come to the Unit One office if we call you. Record your statement.'

I agreed and hung up. My son was home for his Diwali vacation, but a severe bout of jaundice had confined him to bed. I sat with him and held out the many medicines he'd been prescribed.

'Things aren't right,' I told him.

'Why, Ma?'

'Don't worry,' I said. 'We'll be fine. Concentrate on your studies.'

'Okay, Ma.'

'Remember,' I said, 'whatever happens, I will *always* be by your side.'

He moved closer and put his arms around me.

'I'll meet you on 9 December in Panchgani,' I said.

He looked up. 'Promise?'

I kissed his forehead, and a faint smile spread across his sallow face. Later, I confided about the recent developments to my uncle and aunt, who lived next door. They were horrified, but believed in my innocence, and promised to pray for my safety.

On 12 November, Assistant Police Inspector (API) Vilas Datir from the Crime Branch called my number. It was the call I'd been dreading.

'Mahale sir must have spoken to you, madam,' he said.

'Yes,' I said. 'When should I come?'

'By noon,' he said. 'We'll be waiting.'

I had been to the Unit One office at Crawford Market umpteen times over the past five years, especially when I had covered the 26/11 terrorist attacks on Mumbai in 2008. Mahale had played a pivotal role in investigating that attack.

I parked my Hyundai i10. Never had I imagined that I would walk into these premises as a suspect.

Inside Mahale's office, I was asked to sit on a plastic chair. Photos of Lord Ganesha lined the walls. Arun Chauhan, a senior inspector from the Property Cell, took a seat opposite me. Vilas Datir, assistant police inspector, sat down on another table in the same room. He was a tall, imposing man and tapped his heavy fingers on a laptop throughout the interaction.

Chauhan began with the routine questions, asking for details such as my age, and address, which I was sure he already knew. He was only easing me into the questioning, preparing me for what lay ahead.

'Do you know J. Dey's wife?'

'No,' I said.

'Where did he live?'

'I don't know.'

'What about your professional rivalry with him?'

'He was far too senior for such a rivalry to exist.'

Chauhan leaned forward. 'What kind of equation do you share with Chhota Rajan?'

'None whatsoever.'

'But,' he said and showed me an international number written on a piece of paper, 'you've been in regular touch with this number in the last six months, haven't you?'

'Yes,' I said. 'About twenty times in the last six months. That isn't a lot, really.'

'Whom does this number belong to?'

'A friend I met on a social network.'

'How did you meet *him*?'

'Through a common friend. He has no connection to the underworld. His profile can be verified.'

The questioning lasted for three hours, and finally, they let me go. I had kept my bosses at *Asian Age* informed of my trip to Unit One. When I reached the office in the evening, the edit meeting was in progress. Grim faces gathered around me. I clarified that the police were suspicious about a few international calls and that I'd recorded my statement about those. A few colleagues hugged me, and I heaved a huge sigh of relief, thinking that the worst was behind me.

On 14 November 2011, my son returned to his boarding school in Panchgani.

The Crime Branch had not filed a charge sheet yet. Normally, the police are expected to file a charge sheet in court in three months. But under the provisions of MCOCA, they'd requested for an extension, which was granted by the court. The six-month deadline to file the charge sheet was soon approaching. Over the next few days, I also spoke to Himanshu Roy. The conversation put me at ease and strengthened my belief that my fear had been unfounded. On 22 November, I received a call from Binoo Nair, my colleague at the *Asian Age*.

'Where are you?' he asked.

'Home.'

'Oh. Uh . . .' He wanted to say something but could not bring himself to do it. 'Okay, okay.'

'Why, Binoo?' I asked. 'Anything wrong?'

He spoke after an elaborate pause. 'There were rumours at the Press Club that you've been arrested.'

I tried to laugh, only to make him feel better. 'Well, I'm talking to you.'

I hung up soon after, but that call shook me up. And then, two days later, I received a text message from a senior IPS officer. Just two words: 'Stay Strong.'

On the morning of 25 November, I was making some last-minute arrangements for my trip to the Srinathji shrine in Rajasthan. Our train was scheduled to depart at 2.30 p.m. from Bandra Terminus. I was standing with my aunt in the balcony of her home, going over a list of things she wanted me to bring from Rajasthan. A grey Bolero jeep stopped in the narrow lane in front of the balcony. Three lady constables and two heavyset men in safari suits emerged from the vehicle. There was nothing dramatic about their entry, but the purpose behind their trained movements was evident. I rushed back to my flat, which was next door. My grandfather looked up from the newspaper.

'Something wrong?' he asked in chaste Gujarati.

'The police are here.'

'Police? Why?'

My grandfather was a Gandhian who'd lived his entire life with two sets of clothes. His life had been an epitome of simplicity. Confusion loomed large on his face. Before I could explain any further, the cops appeared in the corridor. The lady constable was dressed in plain clothes and wore a *mangalsutra* around her neck.

'Jigna Vora?' she asked.

'That's me,' I said, still in my nightclothes.

'Get dressed,' she said. 'You'll have to come with us.'

'Why?' my grandfather asked.

'Routine questioning,' she said, her tone lowered in some measure. 'She'll be back by evening.'

I knew she wasn't speaking the truth, but I was thankful because it calmed down my grandfather. My mother was bathing, unaware of what was happening. My maid continued cooking in the kitchen, assuming some guests had come over. I walked to my bedroom, and the other lady constable followed. She stayed inside while I changed, and pointed her chin at a photo frame on the walls.

'Who is this boy?' she asked.

'My son,' I said.

She smiled in some measure and waited until I pulled on a pink T-shirt and blue jeans. In a matter of minutes, even before I could bid goodbye to my mother, I was inside the Bolero jeep, sandwiched between the lady constables. On the way from Ghatkopar to Crawford Market, the lady constable asked me to switch off and hand over the Samsung phone I'd recently purchased. At 11.20 a.m., the constables shuffled me inside the Unit One office. API Vilas Datir spoke with a tinge of empathy in his voice.

'Madam,' he said. 'You are under arrest for the murder of J. Dey.'

16

DAYS OF DESTRUCTION

As I sat facing Vilas Datir at the Crime Branch office, I felt strange. The anxiety and turbulent thoughts over the past few weeks had drained me. Now that I sat in that chair, knowing that they had arrested me, my mind had gone numb. So numb that I could collapse that very moment. The enormity of the accusation and the uncertainty that stared at me was yet to sink in.

About fifteen minutes later, when my brain kicked into overdrive, I stared at the sandals on my feet. I had purchased this new pair from the Lord's showroom right opposite the Crime Branch Office a few days ago. I looked at the silver anklets and toe rings I hadn't found the time to take off when the cops had come calling. The sandals hurt like hell.

Why had they arrested me? For what?

The cops, most of whom I had professional dealings with, had stabbed me in my back. Himanshu Roy had assured Zaidi sir that no harm would come my way if I was innocent. I had been through a broken childhood, a broken marriage and just when my career showed promises of a new-found hope, I was pulled to rock bottom again. Why?

I wondered about the situation back home. What were my family members thinking? What about my son? My grandmother had also been taking a bath when the police picked me up. She would have stepped out and found her life changed drastically.

*

Ramesh Mahale called me to his cabin. He couldn't look me in the eyes.

'I had to do my duty.'

'I understand, sir.' I choked and hung my head low. 'But this is a huge mistake.'

'You are allowed one phone call,' he said. 'Seek legal opinion.'

My mobile had already been confiscated on the way to the station. The few cellphone numbers I could dial from memory seemed blurred by my tears. Nobody in my family had the means to deal with such a problem. With great effort, I dialled a number from Mahale's landline with the hope that it would connect to Murtuza Dewan, a friend who had a good network of lawyers. The phone rang endlessly. Just as I was about to hang up, he answered. I was relieved to hear his voice.

'I've been arrested,' I said in Gujarati. 'They are going to produce me in court in a few hours. Need a lawyer.'

'Heard about it,' he said. 'I'm trying to connect with senior advocate Mundargi.'

'The media will be in full strength at the court,' I said. 'Tell my family not to turn up. They won't be able to handle it.'

He agreed, and we disconnected. Ramesh Mahale then asked me to take off all the silver jewellery I was wearing. He also suggested that a constable would go back to my home, and bring over a different pair of clothes because the pink T-shirt and blue jeans I was wearing would not be the right attire for a court appearance. I asked for my asthma inhaler as well. He nodded. I was thankful for this little leniency.

Assistant Commissioner of Police (ACP) Ashok Durape arrived at the office. An ACP-level officer was mandated to produce an MCOCA-accused in court during police custody. Durape also signed my arrest warrant. Mahale asked me to leave his cabin. Half an hour later, a constable returned with a new set of clothes and my inhaler.

The lady officer asked me to change in the bathroom. She warned me not to lock the door. When I protested for my privacy, she stated she would hold the door closed from outside and stand guard. She wanted to make sure I wouldn't escape or attempt suicide. The gents' toilet was stinking. I somehow found a dry corner and changed into a brown kurta and white leggings, and draped a shawl over my shoulders.

Around 2.30 p.m., the police escorted me down the wooden stairs of the Unit One office. As we descended the long staircase, the ground floor was abuzz with activity. Mahale warned me that a huge media contingent was waiting below. I draped the black and white shawl all over my face. 'And for your own good,' he whispered in Marathi, 'don't utter a word on the way out.'

Cameras, mics and voice recorders were thrust into my face. The cameramen and photographers fell over each other and created a stampede-like situation to get a byte. A lady constable pushed me into a waiting Scorpio at the gate. A reporter forced a mic through the window. From the corner of my eye, I realized he was Ganesh Thakur of Star News.

'You have been arrested for the murder of J. Dey,' he said with journalistic urgency. 'What do you want to say?'

I lowered my face into my lap and wailed. What was there to say?

On the way to court, we stopped by GT Hospital at Crawford Market for my medical check-up. A female medical intern asked me if I had any injuries or medical conditions. I informed her of my asthma. After the check-up, we passed by the Metro Theatre and reached the sessions court. The court gates were packed with the media, and the police led me through the back entrance.

But the back entrance was also full of people waiting, and cameras flashed in my face as the police dragged me to the elevator. It clanked its way up to the fifth floor. As the elevator gates opened, more media personnel blocked our way. The police surrounded me and we jostled our way through. All my colleagues from *Asian Age* were waiting in the courtroom. Murtuza was there too. Hussain Zaidi had tears in his eyes.

'Sir!' I screamed out. 'See what they did to me!'

'Keep calm,' he said, trying to control his emotions.

I was ordered to stand beside the witness box. The lady officer held on tightly to my hand. The tension in the air was palpable. Lawyers, policemen, media and the general public had thronged to the court. Dilip Shah was the public prosecutor. He quoted sections to the judge and argued that I had been arrested for emailing J. Dey's details to Chhota Rajan.

Murtuza had engaged another senior advocate, Girish Kulkarni, for my case. Pin-drop silence fell upon the packed court as Kulkarni put forth a brilliant argument. He lambasted the investigation and submitted that there was no concrete ground for my arrest.

But the judge sent me to police custody for four days, until 29 November 2011. My legal team had me sign a *vakalatnama*, which formalized the appointment of my lawyer. It also submitted that I did not wish to make any confession in this case. This would ensure that the police would not extract a confession from me forcefully.

By 3.30 p.m., I was back to the Unit One office. Mahale asked if I wanted to eat something. I merely shook my head. I had had tea in his office countless number of times when reporting on crime stories.

'How about some tea?' he asked now.

'The tea of your police station has turned bitter, sir.'

*

I was asked to sit outside on a chair. But since the media personnel wouldn't stop hounding me, the police shifted me to a small partition where a group of constables were watching TV. The news of my arrest was playing all over. I began crying again. A burly constable stood up from his seat and turned off the television, and I felt thankful for his sensitivity. Around 6.00 p.m., I was informed that I would be shifted to be locked up at Azad Maidan police station. Like a child I pleaded with Mahale not to shift me. But as per the rules, a female accused could not be kept at the Crime Branch after sunset.

'I do not have any more clothes,' I said.

'I'll get a message delivered to your family,' he said. 'You'll be brought back to the Crime Branch first thing in the morning.'

At the Azad Maidan police station, my uncle and cousin were waiting with my clothes. I called out to them but a constable stopped me from meeting them, bringing me back to the reality of my arrest. The clothes were delivered to the police station, a stone building from the British era. An entry was made in the station register. There was one lock-up for females, and a couple more for male accused. I was ushered into the ladies lock-up, which was occupied by two more ladies. The toilet and bathroom were also inside. I hadn't stopped crying. The behaviour of the media hurt me the most. Some kind of karma had ensured that I was getting the same treatment I had subjected others to. I also realized that the media was ruthless enough to relentlessly chase one of their own if it made prime-time news.

One of the ladies in the lock-up had been arrested in a drugs-related case. She tried to console me and offered me the mutton bheja fry that her son had brought for her dinner. I politely refused on account of the fact that I was vegetarian.

I couldn't sleep that night. There was a small window at the top, and I kept trying to look out of it, but there was only darkness. The inhaler eased my breathlessness, but it didn't help a lot. There was enough space in the lock-up, so I kept pacing around the cell thinking of my son. The two women were sound asleep. The dismal stench of the toilet prevented me from going to the toilet until I could find a cleaner place. The next morning, two lady constables asked me if I wanted to bathe.

'Where?' I asked.

They pointed to the same bathroom, which offered no privacy. I decided I would bathe at the Unit One office, which at least had a door.

The Crime Branch cops picked me up at 7.30 a.m. At the Unit One office, the lady officer again asked me not to lock the bathroom door, and diligently stood guard outside. There was no light in this bathroom, and the water was ice-cold. The lady officer allowed me to use the geyser. I took a bath, changed my clothes and stepped out. Later, the same lady officer struck up a conversation with me and expressed astonishment over the possibility of a *patrakaar* killing another.

A tea vendor called Pakya arrived in the office with glassfuls of tea. He knew me from my earlier visits. I called him over.

'Give me a cup of tea,' I said. 'Please.'

He smilingly pulled out a cup from his tray. 'Here.'

'I have no money,' I said. 'I'll pay you later, okay?'

Pakya smiled and went about delivering tea to other policemen. Mahale arrived around 11 a.m. I asked him if I could meet my family members, but the rules did not allow it—he would have to speak to his seniors. Senior Inspector Arun Chauhan from the Property Cell arrived.

'Which email address did you use to communicate with Chhota Rajan?' Chauhan asked me.

'Don't you know already, sir?'

I had answered with my eyes locked into his, unflinchingly. He fell silent. He never asked me another question about the case.

Mahale asked me why I had not informed them about the interview with Chhota Rajan when I was called to give a statement in the J. Dey case. I protested that the question had been twisted. I had been asked if I had any 'relation' with gangsters. The answer was I did not have any, and I still stood by it. Mahale opened his palms towards the various portraits of Lord Ganesha on his walls.

'It is fine if you don't trust me any more,' he said. 'Put your trust in Bhagwan. He will ease things for you.' I nodded.

After sunset, they shifted me back to Azad Maidan. For two days, I hadn't eaten a morsel. The lady arrested in the drugs case asked me to eat again, and again I refused. That night, I put my dupatta on the floor and lay down to give my back some rest. Late in the night, the Crime Branch cops turned up to check on me. They shouted my name and I responded with a grunt, to show that I was alive and hadn't committed suicide or run away.

The next morning, 27 November 2011, I was back at the Crime Branch office. Since it was a Sunday, my neighbour had turned up at the Crime Branch with some food. Mahale allowed me to eat as I hadn't eaten for two days. He also informed me that Hussain Zaidi would come to meet me around 3.30 p.m. We met in Mahale's cabin, in his presence. I asked Hussain Zaidi about the situation outside.

'Pathetic!' he said. 'Media pressure is making it worse.'

'Will our organization support me?'

'Expect nothing,' he said. In his attempt to stand by me, Zaidi sir had published a front-page editorial in the

Asian Age, not knowing that it would eventually cost him his job.

I spoke in a low whisper. 'Should I tell the cops that the Rajan interview was facilitated by Paulson Joseph, the co-accused on the J. Dey murder case?'

'Yes,' Hussain Zaidi said. 'We don't have anything to hide.'

I turned to Mahale, and blurted it out. He was stunned to hear the revelation, but he did not let it show on his face. Paulson had been arrested in this case way before my arrest. His police custody had ended, and he was already in judicial custody. A few minutes later, Hussain Zaidi left and Mahale called me for questioning again.

'What is this angle with Paulson?' he asked.

I explained that I had no direct access to Chhota Rajan. For the interview over the shoot-out at Pakmodiya Street, I had got in touch with one Nishit Chovatiya, who was a resident of Tilak Nagar. I knew him from previous visits to Ganesh mandals in the area. I asked Nishit if he could arrange an interview with 'Nana', which is how Chhota Rajan was referred to. Nishit promised to get back to me in a few days.

He told me I would have to visit Navi Mumbai for the interview, from where Paulson would call Chhota Rajan. On the decided day, Nishit and I drove in his car to Navi Mumbai. At a famous eatery, we were joined by Paulson and Arif. Paulson messaged from his phone a few times, but received no callback. After a long wait, we left the restaurant. Since Nishit and the others were going to south

Mumbai, they decided to drop me at Worli so that I could go to my office at Paragon Centre. Even during the drive, Chhota Rajan did not call back. As I was exiting the car, Arif asked for my number. When I asked for a reason, he said that Chhota Rajan would call me when the time was right. Then, they drove off.

Mahale listened to all of this with complete silence.

'Madarchod Paulson!' he said. 'He never confessed to me about this!'

On Monday, 28 November 2011, the prosecution asked for an extension of my police custody because some new facts had emerged in the case. They also wanted custody of Paulson again, so that they could corroborate his statements with mine. Though I had had no contact with Chhota Rajan before or after the interview, I wondered if I had shot myself in the foot by telling Mahale about Paulson's involvement in the interview. The court admitted the prosecution's submission and granted the required custody for seven days.

By now, the media pressure had reduced a bit. As days passed, reporters stopped showing up as it was no longer Breaking News but had become a routine follow-up story. I could see it in court.

Later in the afternoon, the cops took my fingerprints. They handed me a slate with my name, and I posed for my mugshot. It was the most humiliating experience of my life.

The next day, on Tuesday, my aged grandfather came to meet me at the Crime Branch. He was crying inconsolably and lamented that he was a simple man, with no political connections and no money. I was trying to console him when Aariz Chandra from Aaj Tak arrived. He took a keen interest in snooping on my conversation with my grandfather. Mahale noticed this and asked Aariz to step out. After fifteen minutes of crying, I asked my grandfather to leave because I suspected Aariz would call every possible reporter to create unwarranted sensationalism. I stood by the window and watched my shivering grandfather struggle to keep his walking stick firm. Would I meet him again? My eyes filled with tears when I saw a cameraman pointing a camera at grandfather. My grandfather tried walking faster, but could not because of his age. The camera followed him like a vulture. I kept watching and crying until my ailing grandfather was out of sight.

This routine went on every single day. On 9 December 2011, I switched on the geyser in the dark bathroom of the Crime Branch to take a bath. A loud spark followed, and the stench of fumes filled the air. The lady constable standing guard outside called for me.

'I am okay,' I said, 'but the geyser's dead.'

When I stepped back into the light, I noticed that a purple patch had appeared on my hand as a result of the electric shock. The same day, the court sentenced me to judicial custody.

*

149

During my time in police custody, I was cut off from the world outside. I had gone from being a journalist who chased news to having no idea what was being written about me. Around a week into police custody, when Senior Police Inspector Arun Chauhan of the Property Cell came to the Unit One office, he spoke to me in Hindi about a recent news article.

'Do you know what your friends in the media are saying about you?' he said.

I had no clue.

'They are questioning your lavish lifestyle,' he said. 'Looks like you were a regular visitor to an expensive spa in Ghatkopar.'

'Who wrote this?' I asked.

'A reporter from *DNA*—Priti Acharya,' he said. 'So, you visited the spa once a week?'

'Yes,' I said, refusing to be ashamed of taking care of myself.

'How much does the membership cost?' he asked.

'Rs 35,000 for a year.'

'Pretty expensive, isn't it?'

I sensed the sarcasm in his voice, and clarified that I was a journalist who was earning a decent salary each month by giving her best to her profession and her organization. To spend a portion of my hard-earned money on myself did not make me a criminal, nor could I be forced to feel guilty about that. Nevertheless, I wondered how the reporter in question was able to obtain this information about me. Then,

I remembered that the reporter herself was a member of the same 'expensive' spa—where she would visit for slimming sessions. The services she was undertaking were more expensive than my membership. I had run into her at the spa once. After I was done with my hairstyling, I had offered to drop her to Colaba in my car since I was going down the same route to Crawford Market. During the drive, as we crossed the Wadala Imax, our conversation steered towards my recent trip to Sikkim, and how much I had enjoyed eating momos there. Now, she had reported this conversation like a story about my 'lavish' lifestyle. That night, sitting in the Azad Maidan police lock-up, I realized how an innocuous conversation had been used maliciously against me. Colleagues from my fraternity seemed more than happy to throw me under the bus if it could do them any good.

Savita, a lady constable who was on duty during my police custody, spoke to me about an article in a Marathi newspaper. In a press conference, then commissioner of police Arup Patnaik had made a statement that the MCOCA charges against me could be possibly repealed depending on how the investigation proceeded. The police had arrested me on suspicion of my involvement, but if the investigation suggested otherwise, they may not file a charge sheet against me. This was the essence of the CP's statement.

I had a background in law, and I saw no hope in such red herrings. The CP's words were merely perfunctory, and the entire episode of my arrest was based on weak evidence, which I was determined to disprove in court. But I saw no possibility that the charges would be dropped.

There were two Bohra women from Bandra in the Azad Maidan lock-up with me for a few days. They had been arrested with regard to a different case. They had picked up two copies of a newspaper from a visit to the court and excitedly asked me to read it. The front page carried news of Dev Anand's death. He was an actor I had admired a lot. And then there was a story about me. It said that seven mobile phones had been recovered from Jigna Vora by the police. The article also contained my photo in a yellow T-shirt.

There were other rumours that I was on Chhota Rajan's payroll and had used a satellite phone to contact him. The Bohra women seemed to be in awe of my alleged criminal prowess.

'You had a satellite phone?' one of them asked.

'No,' I said.

'But you had seven mobile phones, yes?'

'No. I had just one phone, which the police confiscated as soon as I was arrested.'

'Why is the media writing all this, then?'

I shrugged. 'Ask them.'

Then one of them looked closely at the photograph and commented that I had brown eyes. I had to disappoint them again by saying I had worn lenses when the photograph was clicked. There was nothing extraordinary about me. But the media had already worked hard to create a different impression.

17

CASTE FACTOR

Among the first few people I got talking to in Byculla Jail was Pooja Thakker. The fact that she was Gujarati created a strange affinity. A few exchanges in my mother tongue soothed me to some extent. Pooja was in her early thirties, fair and very attractive. She introduced herself as a professor of gynaecology from a medical college in Pune. She had already been granted bail and was about to be released in a few days. Before walking out of the jail, she asked if there was any message I wanted to convey to my family. I asked her to tell them that I was coping fine, and that they need not worry about me. She readily agreed to pass on the message, and I gave her my landline number and my lawyer's number.

I was sad to see Pooja leave and lose the one other person around me who spoke Gujarati. But Paromita warned me that Pooja wasn't as angelic as she had portrayed.

Pooja had been arrested for posing as a fake CBI officer and conducting raids. She had allegedly also cheated her prospective in-laws of jewellery worth lakhs. Paromita's warnings made me worry if I had done the right thing by giving her the contact details of my aged grandparents and my mother.

Paromita also told me that Jaya Chheda would often adoringly call Pooja her *bahu rani* (darling daughter-in-law) because of her good looks. She had apparently often expressed her desire to make Pooja her daughter-in-law. Though Pooja and Jaya were not in jail together at the time that I was there, they had met each other before Jaya went away.

The weeks leading up to my first court visit were filled with anxiety. I wanted to speak with my family. And I looked forward to stepping out of the jail and talking to my lawyer Jayesh about the legal strategy. While Girish Kulkarni was the senior counsel, Jayesh was my lawyer for day-to-day hearings. But the thought of facing the world again was too heavy on my mind and morale. What would people think of me now? Would they think I was a murderer? On the day of the court visit, I suffered from severe stomach cramps. It was like I was a child who didn't want to go to school but was forced to. Everyone in the sessions court knew me and held me in high regard—the judges, the lawyers, the peons and even the liftman. How would I ever face them?

As I was an accused under the MCOCA, I was produced in court amidst tight security. The police retinue consisted of six policemen and policewomen in total, including armed guards. As we approached the court building, I saw my aged grandfather sitting on the stairs of the bridge on the fifth floor, which connected the two court buildings. His teary eyes were fixed on the floor. He did not even notice me approaching, but his face lit up when he finally looked up at me. I hugged him tightly and began crying like a baby. A staunch Gandhian, my grandfather was respected in the society for his charitable work. I was guilty of putting him through all this humiliation. But he never castigated me and had only words of comfort for me. In him, I found a pillar of strength. I asked him about my mother and grandmother and was happy to hear that they were fine. I thanked my grandfather for coming to court but pleaded with him not to attend any more hearings because the media had turned up in full force and the pressure of scrutiny would be too much for him to bear.

The hearing lasted barely two minutes, and my judicial custody was extended. On my request, the court allowed me a three-minute call home. The police party accompanied me to a PCO near a Xerox booth. My mother picked up, and she cried on hearing my voice. I told her not to worry about me, and had a brief word with my grandmother too. My pug, Leo, was barking in the background. My mother said that he was aware that they were speaking to me, and was thus getting excited. Leo would roam the house looking for me and yelp sadly when he couldn't find me. I asked my mother to put the phone to his ear. I said a few familiar phrases to Leo. He barked loudly and my mother told me he began licking the receiver. Sadly, the three minutes passed in a jiffy and I had to hang up.

As I was leaving, I asked my grandfather if a lady called Pooja had called. He said she had, and conveyed that she would be happy to carry any message to me in jail, but for money. The conversation did not have a good feel to it. Luckily, my grandfather had discussed the issue with my lawyer, Jayesh, who advised him to tell Pooja that Jigna's lawyer had barred all discussions. As the police car took me back to jail, I promised myself not to trust anyone so easily in Byculla Jail.

18

UNLIKELY SAVIOUR

In January 2009, the Maharashtra Anti-Terrorist Squad arrested IPS officer Saji Mohan in a drug trafficking case. He had been working with the Enforcement Directorate (ED) and Narcotics Control Bureau (NCB). The ATS had apprehended him in Mumbai trying to sell off the very narcotics he had confiscated. It was a big story, and I had visited the ATS office to cover the story. Police officer Pradeep Sawant of the ATS was interrogating Saji Mohan. I sat on a chair and watched the proceedings from a distance. Mohan was seated on the floor, and he was cooperating with his interrogators, readily answering the questions being asked. It was a fall for this IPS officer of the 1995 batch, who had also been conferred with a gallantry medal during his service. I had written several stories on Saji Mohan's lifestyle. To cover up his hair loss, he would wear expensive wigs that allegedly cost around Rs 1.5 lakh each.

In April 2012, I was returning to Byculla Jail from a court visit when I saw considerable police deployment outside the main gate. The policemen were surrounding a bald man. Once I reached the barracks, I asked a constable about the extra security. She informed me that Saji Mohan was being shifted from Arthur Road Jail to Byculla Jail because there was a perceived threat to his life. I had failed to recognize that the policemen were guarding him. His appearance had changed in the years since I had seen him. My immediate thought was, *How would I face him?*, as I had written multiple reports about him while reporting on his drug haul case.

Female inmates were not allowed to interact with male inmates, and their areas were far away from each other. As Saji Mohan was well educated, the prison authorities had assigned him the task of helping the jail doctor, Dr Khan, with maintaining records. I ran into Saji Mohan during a routine visit to the doctor, and as much as I tried to avoid him by fidgeting around the plants, he came up and spoke to me. I thought he would hold a grudge against me for all the stories I had written about him. To my utter surprise, he was very kind and asked about my health. Saji believed I had not committed the crime, and that I should trust the judiciary. I began to weep.

A few weeks later, I met Saji Mohan at the doctor's office again. He used to read the newspapers and had kept a tab on my case.

'Jigna,' he said, 'I read some reports about some transcripts in your charge sheet. Can you tell me about it?'

'Yes,' I said. 'There is a transcript of a conversation between Chhota Rajan and his accomplice, where he claims that I had played a part in instigating him for the murder.'

'If the police obtained these transcripts through telephone surveillance, you must know that orders for such surveillance must be approved by a DIG-level officer or by the additional chief secretary, home. Else, they are illegal.'

I thanked him profusely for the tip and made a mental note to discuss this with Jayesh. I was touched that a policeman whose lifestyle I had left open for everyone to judge was going out of his way to help me. My mind went back to the day at the ATS office when he was sitting on the floor answering questions, and I was sitting on the chair, feeling proud about being a veteran journalist. Today, my pride had been shattered into pieces. And perhaps had also made me a better person.

19

CHEERLEADERS

In the last week of December 2011, I met another inmate named Savita Maushi. She was in her fifties, and had been arrested along with her son for running a prostitution ring in Colaba. There was nothing to do after the daily bandi, so I struck up a conversation with her.

'How long have you been here?' I asked.

'One-and-a-half years,' she said.

'I have never seen you at the barracks before?'

'I was being treated at the J.J. Hospital,' she said. 'They discharged me only a few days ago.'

'Hope all is well now?'

'First class.' She guffawed. 'The government bore responsibility for my heart surgery as I was under arrest. And I saved nearly three-and-a-half lakh rupees on the operation. Being a guest of the state has its own benefits!'

Savita Maushi was rejoicing at her good fortune when a shrill voice echoed in the corridor and a female who looked to be in her twenties emerged, singing and dancing on her way towards the barracks. She was wearing a glittery salwar-kameez, and garish earrings. She strode down the stairs with the confidence of a supermodel walking down a ramp.

Savita Maushi stood up to greet her like she was a close relative. 'My dear Fatima! So nice to see you again.'

Fatima beamed from the other side of the iron bars. 'I am back!'

'Great!' Savita Maushi said. 'Let's catch up tomorrow.'

The cops followed quickly in Fatima's wake and led her to Barrack No. 1 for the night. Savita Maushi told me that Fatima was a thief who had operated in the Cuffe Parade area under the garb of a maid. The next morning, Fatima came to meet everyone in Barrack No. 2. She hugged Paromita like a long-lost friend. Then she came to greet me, and Paromita formally introduced both of us. I took an instant liking to Fatima, because she was laughing and full of joy even inside a depressing place like Byculla Jail.

'Where do you stay, Fatima?' I asked.

'Lalubhai Chawl,' she said. 'You know the area?'

'Of course,' I said. The area was one of the most notorious regions in Govandi, Mumbai, and famous for its pickpockets, thieves, murderers and all kinds of criminals. 'But I was told you operate in Cuffe Parade?'

'Correct,' she said. 'A good thief will never operate in the same area where she lives.'

'Why?'

'Not good for reputation,' she said. Everyone broke out laughing.

'So how come you are back now?' I asked.

'My partner fucked up on a simple job,' she said.

'Really?' I said. 'What happened?'

Apparently, Fatima had been working as a maid and babysitter for an affluent couple who lived on the seventeenth floor of a high-rise in the plush Cuffe Parade area. The couple had two children, aged three and five, whom Fatima would babysit while the parents went about their businesses and jobs. Fatima scanned the house for days, and she knew where the valuables were, what time the kids slept, and when it would be best to make off with the loot. On the day she finalized the robbery, she got one of her friends, Manisha, to help, because the loot was worth at least Rs 10 lakh. Everything went as per plan, except that the five-year-old child happened to wake up early that day. Manisha tried to threaten the kid into silence, which only aggravated the little brat more and he raised an alarm. Fatima managed to escape, while Manisha was caught by the neighbours and handed over to the police. Days later, Fatima was also arrested.

I was amazed at the value of the theft she had attempted. It didn't sound exaggerated because the Cuffe Parade area was known for housing the rich and the wealthy. She explained that the value of the stolen goods was important, because after the robbery, she had to grease the palms of law enforcement agencies and lawyers and a certain portion of the loot also went to the cops as recovery. She would manage to steal from at least five to six homes before getting arrested each time.

'So what happens now?'

'The cops will file a charge sheet,' she said. 'But bail won't be easy unless I give them a greater share of the pie.'

In addition to the relevant sections for robbery, the police had also charged her with Section 326 of Cr.PC which dealt with assault and made the case more serious. Savita Maushi told me that Fatima had made quite a fortune in her profession of choice, and she owned at least four flats in the city and had also invested in a lot of gold and property in her native village. Apparently, she also spent a lot of money on dining at expensive restaurants with her boyfriends. As days passed, Fatima and I began talking more frequently, especially during the night. During one such conversation, she told me that she had three kids, all of them girls, who were now in her mother's care.

'I miss them,' she said. 'And I miss Javed too.'

'Who is he? Your husband?'

'No.' She giggled. 'My boyfriend.'

I gasped. 'You have three children with your boyfriend?'

'No,' she said. 'I divorced the *chutiya* who fathered my children a long time back.'

'What was his name?'

'Saleem,' she said. 'The funny part is that Javed and Saleem were best friends!'

I burst out laughing at her tone. 'How did you get together with Javed?'

She told me that Javed was a rickshaw driver in Govandi, and would visit her home often because he was Saleem's best friend. After she had divorced Saleem, she realized that Javed was interested in her. The exchange of shy glances led her to sit in his rickshaw one day, and off they went to a motel on the outskirts of Mumbai. Inside the motel room, she ordered beer. When she was high enough, she ordered him to take off his clothes. As he stripped, she asked if he had been smart enough to get a condom along. He pulled out a small packet from the pocket of his pants, and held it up for her to see. But there was a problem—Javed had never worn a condom before, and he was nervous. She sat cross-legged on the bed, all naked and ready, and smiling as Javed struggled with the piece of rubber. Finally, she crooked a finger and called him over. And then, she rolled down the condom on him. But her problems did not end there. Javed did not have much experience with women and he struggled to perform in bed. When she finally held him in his hands and guided him inside, he went limp.

'What a put-off!' Fatima told me. 'The behenchod held his useless lauda in his hands and went to sleep.'

I laughed so loudly at the story that a couple of inmates woke up and chided me for disturbing their sleep. I apologized to them, but still could not stop giggling. Questions of morality aside, her manner of telling stories was very funny. She was a woman who loved sex, and was completely unapologetic about it.

Moments like these that made me laugh were few and far between. What amazed me was that Fatima's spirit was not broken despite her situation. A few nights later, she began narrating another incident to me.

'After numerous attempts, Javed got better with fucking, but I decided not to waste my hard-earned money on hotel rooms.'

'Then where did you make out?'

'In his rickshaw.'

My jaw almost hit the floor. 'What!'

'Yes,' she said. 'But even that was a disaster.'

'Why?' I asked.

She told me that Javed drove her to a deserted road in Trombay. The area is located on the outskirts of Mumbai, and sparsely populated. He parked the rickshaw somewhere in the vicinity of Bhabha Atomic Research Centre, one of India's premier nuclear research facilities. Javed had a different sort of research on his mind. He wanted to have anal sex. Fatima was fairly open to the idea because, according to her, he wouldn't need to put on a condom. So they undressed and tried to get intimate on the back seat of the rickshaw. But Javed had underestimated the difficulty of anal sex. The entire rickshaw shook with the effort. Fatima turned and scorned him, and that was all it took for him to go limp again.

'I told the motherfucker to never show me his lauda again,' Fatima told me. 'But even he was addicted to sex now. For the next three days, we fucked in all different places.'

'And what happened on the fourth day?'

'The police arrested me for the botched job at Cuffe Parade,' she said and laughed.

Often during our late-night conversations, Fatima would speak about her active sex life. What was the first thing she wanted to do after she got bail? Nobody in Byculla Jail had a problem guessing that.

In January 2012, a heavily pregnant inmate called Vinita was moved to Barrack No. 2. She was Fatima's friend, and also an old-timer at Byculla Jail. She had been in and out on various charges over the past ten years. She also lived in Govandi, but operated in the Juhu area, living by the code of conduct of thieves, which meant everyone stuck to their designated areas. Fatima also swore by the code.

She was about thirty years old, but looked beyond her years because of the various pregnancies she had been through. She had borne at least six children, and had undergone an equal number of abortions. She giggled like a college-going girl and confessed that none of her children had the same father.

'What was your biggest job?' I asked her.

'I once worked at Parveen Babi's home,' she said.

'The Bollywood actress?' I said. 'You looted her home?'

'Not hers. She was confined to a wheelchair but she kept a close watch on me. At the slightest hint of suspicion, she would create a ruckus. So I looted one of her neighbours.'

'How much?'

Her chest swelled with pride. 'Rs 20 lakh.'

Later, Fatima told me that Vinita also spent a lot of her money on the men she loved. She was fond of eating at the best restaurants of the city. She delivered a baby in January 2012, and was out from jail around July 2012. However, she was arrested again for a crime and was back in Byculla Jail by August 2012. Now, she had a six-month-old baby with her. And she was pregnant again! Nobody was surprised.

Simran had been in jail when I was locked up. She was hardly eighteen or nineteen years old, but already famous in her line of work—stealing mobile phones. She lived in Mira Road in a one-bedroom flat, but her area of operation was Malad railway station, which was heavily crowded between 8.00 a.m. and 10.00 a.m. with people rushing to office. She would wear a burqa and position herself in front of the first-class ladies compartment. She would choose her victims by the clothes they wore. Her preferred choice was the girls who wore cropped tops and expensive jeans, and worked in affluent call centres in Malad. It was most likely that such women had high-end mobile phones in their purses or pockets. In a flash, Simran would stealthily flick the phone, switch it off and put it inside her purse before vanishing into the sea of people at the station, which was made easier by her short and slim demeanour. The hapless victims did not even realize their phone had been flicked until the train left the station.

'What would you do with the phones you stole?' I asked.

'I sold them to a shop in Malad east. The shop owner would destroy the SIM card and pay me in cash, on the spot.'

'How much did you usually make?'

She smiled, displaying a chipped tooth in the corner of her mouth. 'About 50,000 rupees a day.'

Simran loved shopping in the big malls of Malad. She was also a regular at a very famous pub in suburban Mumbai. All these girls who stole for a living displayed a deep understanding of human psychology. She did not work on the weekends, because offices were shut. Simran had also chosen Malad railway station as her zone of operation because office-goers did not report theft as they feared the hassles of engaging with the police. Since the crime was committed on the railway platform, it fell under the jurisdiction of the Railway Protection Force, which is not the most motivated crime-fighting unit. Most of her victims did not even come back to search for their lost phones, and simply gave up hope of recovering the device, while Simran made a fortune. When I met her, she was pregnant, but she steered clear of discussions that veered close to the identity of her husband.

'Whom do you stay with?' I asked her.

'I stay alone,' she said. 'My family stays in Uttar Pradesh.'

Later, Fatima told me that Simran was heavily into drugs and boyfriends. Jocularly, she went to the extent of calling Simran 'characterless' because she felt Simran was having an affair with her husband's friend. When I questioned Fatima about her similar escapades with Javed, Fatima took great pride in explaining that all her sexual encounters with Javed had happened only *after* her divorce with Saleem.

'Unlike Simran, I never two-time my men,' Fatima said and laughed.

*

Milee was a good-looking girl who had been arrested in August 2011, prior to my arrest. Her father had passed away, while her mother and younger brother lived in Odisha. Hardly twenty, she used to work in a factory in her village.

'My mother and I had an argument,' she said. 'So I just boarded a random train, and it brought me here.'

'Did you have any money when you left home?'

'About 5,000 rupees,' she said.

'And did you know anyone in this city?'

'No.'

'How did you find a place to live, then?'

'The autorickshaw driver who picked me at Kurla station guided me to an area near Powai.'

'And how did you get arrested?'

Milee had found a job as an assistant to a hairdresser on the sets of a TV serial. She would travel to work by bus every day, and noticed that a boy would board the same bus as her, and was displaying an interest in her. Eventually, they fell in love and he also began picking her up from work every day. On the way back home, they would sit on the last seat of the bus. Her boyfriend would often fondle her breasts and kiss her when he thought no one was watching.

He was the one who devised a new idea of making money. Late in the nights, in the JVLR area, Milee would wear skimpy clothes and lure unsuspecting men to isolated areas with the promise of sex. Moments later, her boyfriend would arrive and they would attack the victim and make off with money and valuables. The con was eventually busted, and Milee got arrested, while her boyfriend escaped.

One night, Milee asked me if I had a boyfriend. I was single then, but Milee refused to believe me. She had heard from other inmates that I was having an affair with Himanshu Roy, who had been instrumental in my arrest. I had no idea how to answer that, but her questions never stopped.

'Didi,' she asked me, 'what is rape?'

I was aghast. 'What happened, Milee? Did someone force you?'

'No,' she said. 'I am only curious to know.'

I explained the meaning of the term to her, and she listened intently.

'Didi,' she said, 'I want to experience rape once.'

Disconcerted and frustrated, I blurted, 'Have you gone mad?'

'What difference would it make if my boyfriend raped me?' she said and laughed. 'We have had sex so many times.'

Milee was hopeful that her boyfriend would bail her out. She often returned dejectedly from court hearings at Borivali, because her boyfriend did not turn up to help her. I could completely relate with that, because none of my friends showed up to support me too. Every time I was taken to court, my eyes turned towards a high-rise building that stood on the way from Byculla Jail to Kala Ghoda court. A friend I'd known for years lived in that building, on the fourth floor. I would expect him to be present in court, for nothing else but moral support. But like so many others, he failed to turn up. However, Milee's faith in her boyfriend never wavered. Eventually, he turned up, and Milee got bail. Her smile that day filled me with hope.

20

THE BIRTHDAY GIFT

I turned thirty-seven on 21 February 2012, the day the police filed a charge sheet against me.

Since my arrest in November, they had been racing against time to file a charge sheet against me. As per the Indian Penal Code, the police have to file it within three months. But since the Crime Branch had pressed MCOCA charges against me, they could ask the court for gradual extensions up to a maximum of three additional months. Using the same strategy, the Crime Branch had filed the first charge sheet against the ten accused on 3 December 2011, about six months after J. Dey's murder. The reasons cited for these extensions included the delay in processing the forensics reports, ongoing investigations, and post-mortem reports, etc.

My name was not included in the first charge sheet. The police decided to file a supplementary charge sheet against me at a later stage. I was accused of providing Chhota Rajan with J. Dey's photograph, phone number and office and home addresses. But during the course of the investigation, the police also came up with the notion that I had instigated Chhota Rajan to kill J. Dey.

My legal recourse ultimately depended on the charge sheet. Even though the Crime Branch had conducted elaborate press conferences to detail my involvement in the murder, none of that was admissible in a court of law. The charge sheet thus became the most important document because then the police would be going on record to say what I was accused of and the evidence they had to prove the charges.

On one hand, I had to worry about the charge sheet, while on the other, I had to focus on surviving life in jail. Life in Byculla Jail was torturous. At first, I hoped and prayed to get bail. But as days turned into months, I dreaded getting bail because I was frightened to face the world outside. It sent shivers down my spine to think about answering questions and facing suspicious stares. My career and reputation had been destroyed.

Jayesh Vithlani, my lawyer, would meet me regularly at Byculla Jail. He would brief me on the progress of the case, and always advise me to be patient. My uncle and a cousin brother would also come to meet me, and they would keep me posted about the world outside the walls of the prison. I often asked Jayesh if the police were going to ask for an extension to file the charge sheet because that would mean a further delay in my bail. He did not have an opinion on that.

The police had confiscated my personal laptop, the hard disk from the desktop I used at the *Asian Age* office, and my cellphone. The forensic reports of these devices were still pending. I was worried that the police would plant evidence against me. Mostly, I feared that they would plant J. Dey's photograph, or that of his bike, in my devices, and claim that I had it stored.

Incidentally, months before I had been arrested, I was passing by Amar Mahal Junction on my way to Chembur and happened to notice a high-end sports bike parked outside a shop. I had clicked a photograph of that shining, yellow two-wheeler only to show it to my son, who was extremely fond of imported bikes. I became paranoid that the police would use this against me. Even in custody, I had confessed to Inspector Ramesh Mahale that I had a photograph of a bike on my phone but that bike did not belong to J. Dey.

My fears may sound like hysteria now, but the fact was that the police had arrested me in a case where I had no involvement, and there was no reason why they would not use unfair means to have me convicted.

I had a purchased an Apple MacBook before my arrest, and I had not even learnt to operate it properly before I was put behind the bars. This was the laptop that they had confiscated. There was no question about finding J. Dey's photograph on my laptop. But I had lots of Hindi songs from the 1970s and '80s on my hard disk, mostly by Mohammad Rafi and Kishore Kumar, and composed by R.D. Burman. There were some personal photographs from a visit to Bangkok in 2010, a junket that came from the office. We had been staying in a resort, and some photographs in the swimming pool, of me wearing a swimming costume. I feared the police would leak these to the media.

The police had accused me of emailing J. Dey's details to Chhota Rajan. They had shot off a letter rogatory to Google to obtain the emails in question from my gmail account. I often wondered if the police could hack into my account and create the evidence they wanted. I prayed fervently, calling upon God to undo the wrong that had been done to me.

I also wanted to know who had recorded false statements against me, and that would only be clear once the charge sheet was filed. The police had pulled out my CDRs (call detail records) from my telecom operator. Though I was nowhere connected to the crime, my personal life was all out in the open. The police knew whom I was dating, what I was eating, what I was shopping for, and every other possible detail. I was also worried about the safety of my family and friends with whom I had spoken regularly, for the police could frame whomever they wanted to.

While in custody, I was taken to court every fourteen days, but apart from my lawyer and family members, none of my friends came to meet me. Around fifteen people from my family, including my uncles and aunts, would turn up for each of my court visits without fail. Despite this, the media floated reports that my family had disowned me. In Byculla Jail, Jaya Chheda spared no opportunity to dampen my spirits further. She was sure that Ramesh Mahale, who was the investigating officer for her case and mine, would file such a strong charge sheet against me that I would languish in jail for ever.

Jayesh informed me that rumours were afloat that the police would allow my discharge from the case on 10 February 2012, since no incriminating evidence had been found against me. I began praying fervently again, praying for my luck to turn around. Usually, I was produced in court surrounded by the usual security of two women constables armed with rifles, two unarmed women constables, two male constables and one inspector. People charged of crimes under the MCOCA were always provided with this kind of security cover so that they did not escape under any circumstance. It was one of the most humiliating experiences of my life, for I was treated like a terrorist. However, my fellow inmates took great pride in this arrangement because they thought my security was on par with that of a minister. Fatima lamented the fact that the male constables who accompanied her to court were so frail that they would not even get an erection!

When the day arrived, surrounded by the policemen, I walked into the court at Kala Ghoda. Courtroom number 56 on the fifth floor was jam-packed with media personnel. My hopes of freedom were dashed again when Raja

Thakare, the public prosecutor, informed the judge that the charge sheet had been sent to the police commissioner's office for sanction before it could be produced in the court. This meant that eventually, the charge sheet would be filed and I would not be discharged. As a crime journalist, I knew Raja Thakare professionally, and he had given me quite a few leads on the Telgi scam. This added to my humiliation because now he had the job to ensure I stayed behind bars. He acknowledged my presence with a nod of his head. Ten days were additionally provided to the prosecution, and 21 February 2012 was fixed as the next date for my court visit.

My paranoia reached its peak in these ten days because now the trial was a certainty. I had also developed a psychological aversion to the court, and my stomach would ache uncontrollably every time a court visit was due. On the day of the visit, I would have to use the filthy toilet multiple times to ease myself. I even stopped eating to avoid this situation, but it didn't help.

On 21 February, the court was packed again with media personnel. Crime Branch officers arrived with a big, white bag made of jute and produced the charge sheet before Judge S.M. Modak. Jayesh was not available on that day. Later, Raja Thakare told me to hold on to my faith in God. Since it was my birthday, my father's elder brother had brought a piece of pastry for me, and the court granted them permission to give it to me. I choked as I put a spoonful of that cake in my mouth. My uncle had always been fond of me since childhood. If I ever wanted a toy, he was the one I would rush to. When I was a barely six years old, I asked him to bring me a VCR from Dubai so that I could watch Amitabh Bachchan's 1976 movie *Hera Pheri* on TV. He brought me a 'National' VCR, which was a favourite amongst those who worked in the Middle East. This was the first time he had come to see me since my arrest, and he was crying inconsolably. My only thought at that moment was to prove my innocence in this case.

After returning to Byculla Jail, around 8.30 p.m., I was watching Doordarshan on the small TV when the news anchor read a report of a charge sheet being filed against me. Some of the most thickened criminals in the city turned to stare at me. I had no idea where to look!

The next morning, a newspaper chose to carry headlines saying the Crime Branch had gifted the charge sheet to me for my birthday. One news story stated that I had exchanged thirty-three calls with Chhota Rajan. I was stunned. The headlines only accentuated my fears that the police had tampered with evidence because I had only spoken to Chhota Rajan *once*—for an interview over the Pakmodiya Street shoot-out in May 2011, wherein two shooters had gunned down Iqbal Kaskar's driver to death. Iqbal was Dawood Ibrahim's brother, and their gang had been warring with Chhota Rajan's ever since the two had parted ways around 1993. During the course of his interview, Chhota Rajan had only called me thrice on the same day. The first two calls lasted barely five seconds and had got disconnected. The third call was the actual interview. This story was already in the public domain. How the number of calls changed from three to thirty-three was beyond my wildest imagination! There was another story that said that Paulson, another accused in the J. Dey murder case, had confessed about my involvement. But Paulson had been arrested way before me, and his confession had also been recorded much earlier, when there had been no mention of my name.

Three days later, Jayesh delivered a 3,000-page charge sheet to me in jail. The sheer bulk of the document frightened me. All the inmates were astonished that a supplementary charge sheet had run into 3,000 pages. At night, when other inmates were asleep, I went about studying the charge sheet. I started turning page after page to search for the mention of thirty-three calls between Chhota Rajan and me. But even after I reached the last page, there was no such statement in the charge sheet. So, the media had cooked up this story on their own, or it had been maliciously fed to them. And they had lapped up these false reports and printed them without a thought of the damage it would cause to me. They never bothered checking my charge sheet either. All these reports were published 'according to sources'. My own judgement was that this source was Himanshu Roy. He had been present when Hussain Zaidi, the editor of the *Asian Age*, had met then home minister R.R. Patil in connection with my case. Himanshu had made a similar statement at that time.

As I scoured through the charge sheet, I realized that most of the pages were filled with telecom CDRs of my number and those of the witnesses. The statements of various witnesses covered barely forty pages. Some statements were from the cops themselves, who were present for the *panchnama* of my arrest, and for the confiscation of my laptop and mobile phone.

The charge sheet made no mention of any email exchanges between Chhota Rajan and me. Chhota Rajan's email ID was also not mentioned in the email. I made my notes and observations on the blank sides so that I could discuss them with Jayesh later. Even the letter rogatory to Google did not reveal any suspicious emails.

Four reporters had recorded their statements in the charge sheet. Their names had been masked with white ink so that I would not attempt to influence them during the trial. I tried figuring out the names by reading their statement.

The first reporter had received a call from Chhota Rajan on 30 June 2011, in which Chhota Rajan claimed responsibility for J. Dey's murder. Chhota Rajan had explained that J. Dey had turned traitor and was spying for Dawood Ibrahim, and thus, he had been eliminated. There was nothing incriminating against me in this statement. I figured this reporter was Sunil Singh of NDTV.

The second statement was recorded by Jitendra Dikshit of Star News (later ABP). This call happened on 16 November 2011, and the conversation was not too different from the first. Again, there was no mention of my name.

Apparently, Chhota Rajan had called the third reporter around the first week of September 2011, when the same story had been repeated, but the reporter had asked Chhota Rajan if someone had provided him with the registration number of J. Dey's bike, photograph and addresses. Chhota Rajan merely said that one of his acquaintances had sent those details, and hung up. Then, allegedly, Chhota Rajan had called him again after two days and said that Jigna Vora had provided the mentioned details that had helped J. Dey's killers identify their victim.

It was easy for me to figure out statements from Sunil Singh and Jitendra Dikshit because their interviews with Chhota Rajan were available in the public domain. To identify the third witness, I checked the CDRs of the witnesses to make a logical connection. No reporter had a direct line to Chhota Rajan. If an interview or conversation had to be scheduled, the reporter would have to connect to an intermediary known to Chhota Rajan, and then Chhota Rajan would call the reporter at a scheduled time from a VOIP number that ended in 444 or 441. It took me two long nights, but I found the mobile number that had received such a call in the first week of September. The number belonged to Aariz Chandra, who worked for Aaj Tak. Aariz I thought had turned sour because he had once asked me for the letters that Monica Bedi had written to Abu Salem, but I had politely refused for professional reasons. Since that day, it had felt like a cold war had started between us. I noted this down for Jayesh to bring up as an argument for my case.

Case no: RC1(S)–2016–SCU–V–SC–II–CBI–New Delhi
Original case no: 19–2012
Aariz Chandra's statement given to CBI on 29-03-2016 as under Section 161 of Cr.PC:

I am as above. I shifted in above address with my mother and sister only last month. I am graduate of Mumbai University and working as News reporter. I am employed as a senior correspondent with the hindi news channel viz Aaj tak. I am tasked with collection of information regarding criminal activities in Mumbai and to submit this news items in the office. I know almost all the reporters from all print media and electronic media in Mumbai area. While I was working with the sahara news channel I got acquainted with senior correspondent Mr. Jyotirmay Dey. He had a very good knowledge of underworld crime in Mumbai. While exchanging news information we became friends.

On 11-06-2011, I had weekly off and while I was at home, I received a call from reporter friend that there was a firing on Mr. dey at Powai and he got killed. Thereafter on 12-06-2011, I attended the funeral of Mr. Dey at Rajawadi crematorium. On 25-06-2011 Crime Branch Mumbai arrested some of the accused persons in connection with the above crime and held press conference I attended the same. In the said press conference police claimed that on the instructions of Chhota Rajan his associates from the gang had killed Mr. dey

I further state that some time in the last week of August or first week of September, in the afternoon, I received a phone call on my mobile phone number 98******44 from number +3444. As I picked up the call the caller said 'I am Nana calling. I knew that in the underworld Chhota Rajan is known by the nickname as 'Nana'. So also I had heard Chhota Rajan's interview on the TV and identified the caller to be Chhota Rajan. As such I realized that the caller was Chhota Rajan himself and replied, 'Yes nana speak.' Thereafter Chhota Rajan said that, 'he wanted to inform that J. Dey was not a nice person. He became friendly with D company. He had betrayed me. He had published misleading news about me. I was called to meet him in London, but my Dubai based contact informed me that there could be threat to my life, as such I did not go. Thereafter he called me to Phillipines. But I had my doubts, hence I got him killed. I told Chhota Rajan 'killing him was not the solution'. On this he quipped that 'he was conniving with the traitors and providing them my information.' Thereafter I asked Chhota Rajan as to who gave him details, address and motorcycle number of JDey. On this he replied 'he was provided this information by his men'. He also said

'D' company had a hand in July blast in Mumbai. I have conveyed this information to police through my sources. I asked him whether he would give interview on this issue, to which he said 'the information is being worked out, I would call later on.' So saying he disconnected the call.

Next day again in the evening between 1800 hrs–1900 hrs, I received a call from +3444, caller from the other side said 'I am Nana calling.' I immediately recognized the voice as that of Chhota Rajan and replied 'Nana speak up.' Chhota rajan then said as 'as Jdey was working hand in glove with the traitors, I had killed him, I was provided with the details by Jigna Vora through mails, jigna vore had given information of Jdey's motorcycle, photograph, phone numbers and residential address through emails, I again asked him whether he would like to give interview about this.He declined and disconnected the call.

Apart from above, I also want to add that except this interview, Chhota Rajan never interviewed by me. I don't have his numbers, the calls were originated from him only. I don't know from whom he got my mobile number, I did not record this interview and also this interview was not aired because before this he had already told this to many reporters and some of them even aired the same on TV.

The statement was over and explained to me in Hindi and found to be correctly recorded.

The last statement in the charge sheet was from Nikhil Dixit, who was very close to J. Dey and had even performed his last rites. He had allegedly received a call from Chhota Rajan, in which no mention was made about me. But apparently, when Nikhil was learning the ropes of investigative journalism, J. Dey had spoken of a professional rivalry that existed between him and me. The evidence of this was an SMS sent in Marathi, allegedly from me to J. Dey, which J. Dey had shown to Nikhil. The message read, *'Tu swatala shana samajhto kaay'* ('You think you are too smart?').

I made a counter-argument that I was a Gujarati and J. Dey was a Bengali. Both of us were working for English newspapers. Why would I send him an SMS in Marathi?

Then there was a statement from a certain Manoj Shivdasani. He had received a call from Chhota Rajan on 2 August 2011, which was tracked by the police. The transcript of this call was available in the charge sheet. Here, Chhota Rajan lamented that Vinod Chembur had been arrested in the case for identifying J. Dey to his murderers. And then Chhota Rajan claimed that I had complained to him about J. Dey multiple times.

Transcripts as filed in charge sheet.
Date: 4 August 2011. Time: 14.20.10

Manoj: Hello

Chhota Rajan: Haan Manoj

Manoj: Ha

Chhota Rajan: Kya haal hai raja? Uss din cut ho gaiya

Manoj: Haan, haan abhi iska tabiyat thik nahi hai, tabiyat toh thik nahi hai abhi uska bhi, Vinod ka

Chhota Rajan: Kya karega raja, bahut taklifwalli, yeh toh khota phas gaiya

Manoj: Haan

Chhota Rajan: Galat phas gaiya aur who bhi bhenchod, who bhi koi saav nahi tha, who bhi haramipaana who bhi samnewale k liye kaam karta tha dawood k liye ISI k liye

Manoj: Acha acha

Chhota Rajan: Galat galat baatein apne liye . . . likhta tha aur kafi iske matlab jo inke editor log bhi patrakar log bhi iske against kafi the

Manoj: Hmmm . . . mmm

Chhota Rajan: Kafi log iske against bolte the, who kya iska naam who ladki bhi phone kar k mereko bolti thi yeh gadar hai

Manoj: Acha

Chhota Rajan: Who Jigna vora kon hai na

Manoj: Woh malum nahi

Chhota Rajan: Woh hai na

Manoj: Haan haan

Chhota Rajan: Who kafi log matlab iske against the, who jigna vora ghadi ghadi bolti thi, who aisa hai, who waisa hai matlab samnewale k touch main hai na

Manoj: Acha acha

Chhota Rajan: Toh mai jaane ka koi matlab tha nahi, phir Phillipines bula raha tha aur gal matlab chalo koi level hoti hai bhai matlab ek insaan

Manoj: Hu . . . hu . . .

Chhota Rajan: Patrakar hai kuch likh te hai, matlab who toh main bhi samajta hu na

Manoj: Haan haan

Chhota Rajan: But kisi k liye kaam kare aur kisi k lie ekdum hi galat tarike se niche utar k bole toh who galat hai na

Manoj: Thik hai

Chhota Rajan: . . . Matlab kya hai halat bura hai, matlab bahut taklif ho gayi actually matlab na

Manoj: Haan

Chhota Rajan: Yeh khota phas gaiya hai, khota

Manoj: Haan

Chhota Rajan: Tha lena dena kuch nahi iska

Manoj: Haan who toh hai, tabiyat bahut kharab hai

Chhota Rajan: . . . Tabiyat toh bechare ki bahut wohi mere ko bahut bura lag raha hai na, ki kya kare matlab na? aisa phas gaiya thik hai dekhte hai raja koshish karo aur kya?

Manoj: Ok

Chhota Rajan: Ok

Manoj Shivdasani's statement was recorded in the presence of a magistrate under Section 164 of Cr.PC. In his statement, he alleged that Chhota Rajan had also told him about receiving an email from Jigna Vora with J.

Dey's photograph, bike registration number and addresses. However, there was no such record in the transcript of the only conversation between Shivdasani and Chhota Rajan. It clearly implied that Shivdasani's testimony was false.

In the charge sheet, there was a letter from Senior Police Inspector Sripad Kale addressed to Deven Bharati, additional commissioner, crime. This letter was written on 1 August 2011. Kale had requested Bharati for permission to put a number under surveillance as the number belonged to a certain 'Raj' who was using it for making threatening calls. This number was the same as the one used by Shivdasani to speak with Chhota Rajan. Now, such a permission could only be granted by a DIG-level officer, or by the additional chief secretary, home. But the police had recorded that call the very next day and the letter was written only later, which actually made the tapping illegal.

There was no forensic lab report in the charge sheet. Public Prosecutor Raja Thakare had advised the court that the FSL report would be made available as soon as the forensic investigations are complete.

To debunk the theory that I instigated Chhota Rajan to murder J. Dey, I noted that my only conversation with Chhota Rajan happened on 25 May 2011, which was an interview given to my newspaper over the Pakmodiya Street shoot-out. Chhota Rajan had claimed responsibility for this incident, and cited the example of his 'patriotic don' image. He was particularly vocal about conducting an operation in Dawood Ibrahim's area.

Now, to support the instigation theory, the Crime Branch claimed that on 30 June 2011, I had allegedly emailed two articles to Chhota Rajan. J. Dey had written these articles to highlight Chhota Rajan's diminishing influence in the underworld, which, according to them, instigated the don to eliminate the reporter who was bad-mouthing him. But no conversation had taken place between Chhota Rajan and me after the interview I had conducted with him. Also, the first charge sheet that the police filed against the ten accused had contained a confession of accused Arun Dhake. Dhake had confessed that the gun used in J. Dey's murder was procured in Nainital, from one Deepak Sisodia, around 8 May 2011. The shooters had returned to the city on 19 May 2011. So, the conspiracy to murder had already been hatched way before I could instigate Chhota Rajan on 30 June 2011, even if that was true.

For the sake of argument, let's assume that Chhota Rajan had a change of heart after 19 May 2011 and he had dropped the idea to kill J. Dey, but then my alleged emails on 30 June 2011 instigated him to go ahead with the original plan. Even in this case, there were no records, no emails or phone calls or any kind of contact established between Chhota Rajan and me after 25 May 2011. So how could I have instigated him?

When Jayesh came to meet me in Byculla Jail, I had all my counter-arguments ready. Diligently, I dictated each of these points to him, which he jotted down in his black diary. He was convinced we were on the right track. The FSL report was still a loose end, and I feared that the police would try to manipulate it. Jayesh suggested that we engage the services of a senior counsel to apply for bail. It would involve a hefty fee, but Sudeep Pasbola would be the senior advocate who would fight to get me out of jail.

21

CHEATS

Jo Sat Baar Paath Kar Koi, Chhutahi Bandi Maha Sukh Hoi. Whoever recites this *Hanuman Chalisa* 100 times daily for 100 days is freed from the bondages of life and death, and enjoys eternal bliss.

My aunt believed the *Hanuman Chalisa* would form a protective *kavach* (armour) around me in jail. The hymn proved to be a great source of strength during my ordeal. Around 3.30 p.m. every day, I would sit by the veranda and chant these lines with vigour. A huge tree stood in the compound, which was some distance away, but I could not recognize its variety. The leaves on its branches had withered away. The tree was just like me. Once it had been filled with life, but now it was barren. The seeds of spirituality made me understand that these cycles of degeneration would be followed by regeneration, and my life would also be restored in the same manner. Other inmates started following my lead and would join me at the veranda to recite their prayers every day. I often thought of us as birds who flocked together in the hope of flying away from this cage.

Byculla Jail could turn the staunchest sceptics into believers. I come from a Vaishnava family. We are followers of Lord Krishna, and members of the Krishna Panth sect. When I was young, my grandmother never allowed me to visit a Shiva temple because I wasn't married then. I had never recited the *Hanuman Chalisa* at home because Hanumanji is a *brahmachari*. But in jail, I broke all the rules that my grandmother had implemented so strictly and sought divine assistance from Hanumanji.

*

Certain inmates were entitled to hot water for a bath, and Paromita would keep a mug of water from this bucket stored in her thermos to make some coffee later in the day. One morning, she called me over and handed me a cup of Nescafe.

'Jigna,' she said. 'You should chant the mantra of Bagalamukhi Devi.'

She understood from the look on my face that I had not heard of the deity yet. But I was prepared to do anything that could secure my release. Before my arrest, I remembered laughing at a news story that Sheena Bora, who was accused in a high-profile murder case, had performed a maun vrat. Now, I was doing all the same things, and none of it seemed ludicrous.

'What is the procedure for that mantra?' I asked.

'Read it eleven times a day. But be extremely careful,' Paromita said. 'Fumbling in the recitation will negate your wishes.'

'Give me the mantra, please.'

'I wrote it for Asha Pardeshi, who is lodged in Barrack No. 5. Collect it from her.'

'Please write it for me now.'

'I am not in the mood,' she said, and walked away.

The same afternoon, a woman in her fifties came and sat next to me in the veranda. She was a plump lady, wearing a neatly draped sari. Her hair had greyed, and I had seen her shuffle around on wobbly knees. A blue scarf covered her head.

'Are you Jigna Vora?' the woman asked.

I nodded.

'What are you reading, beta?'

'*Hanuman Chalisa*,' I replied. 'What are you reciting?'

'Bagalamukhi Mantra.'

'Oh,' I said. 'Are you Asha Pardeshi from Barrack No. 5?'

'Yes.'

'Thank God,' I exclaimed. 'Paromita asked me to get the Bagalamukhi Mantra from you.'

Since Asha knew the mantra by heart, I ran to get a pen and paper from the barrack. I had this irrational fear that

Asha would refuse to give me the mantra later, and I would rot in jail for ever. But thankfully, she was still sitting in the veranda when I returned, and I managed to write down the mantra.

*

The cops kept their distance from me due to my journalistic credentials. Neither did they harass me a lot, nor did they allow me a lot of liberty, but it was a fine arrangement that kept me out of trouble. I had never performed puja at home, but every morning in jail I would spend an hour, from 9.30 a.m. to 10.30 a.m., chanting various mantras and invoking the gods. None of the inmates disturbed me during this puja time. A baba had told my grandfather that I should recite 'Om Namah Shivaya' for an early release. My grandfather sent me a *tulsi mala* (necklace of holy basil beads), and I would recite it 108 times in five cycles every day. I would light incense sticks, and pray to Lord Shiva and Lord Krishna. This was the best use of my time, and it helped me connect to my inner self. I also began participating in all religious practices performed in Byculla Jail—even those that crossed the line of superstition or stemmed from other religions. Sometimes, I did not even sip water on nights of the full moon. I learnt to recite a few *dua*s (prayers) from the Muslim inmates. All of this gave me some hope to cling to.

Asha and I became good friends. When the barracks were opened each morning, Asha would come down to Barrack No. 2 to meet me as soon as she could. Sometimes, I would go to her barrack. We would often cut vegetables for the meals and talk about our lives. Jailers used to assign us various tasks, such as cutting vegetables, cleaning rice, and separating wheat and chaff. It was a good way of killing time. Seeing the worms in the vegetables, we were thankful to have a chance to be able to cut out the spoiled parts. When I narrated my case to Asha, she was sure that I was innocent. On my inquiring about her case, she revealed that she had been arrested for committing a fraud of Rs 25 crore. Apparently, a chit fund that she had started with her husband for the dhobis (washermen) who lived near Dhobi Talao had gone bust. I remembered reading this in the newspapers before my arrest. Asha, a native of Uttar Pradesh, lived at Mahalakshmi with her husband, Ramesh, who was a very good cook and into the catering business. Asha swore that she had no intention of cheating the laundry men. Everything was going well, and her investments had ensured good payments to those who had given her money. She had even opened an office near Arthur Road. But at some point, she messed up, and things got out of hand. She had every intention to repay the dhobis, and had even sold her land in UP and all her jewellery for that purpose. Her requests to the dhobis about not filing a police case yielded no result, and the police had arrested her and her husband. She often cried, and reiterated that she was not running a scam.

Even though my rational mind could see ponzi written all over her scheme, in my heart I felt she was innocent. Because I had been framed, I was inclined to believe each woman in Byculla Jail was innocent. The police could ruin anyone they wanted to. After the arrest of an accused, the media only covers what the police have to say. And unlike the police, most accused do not have the liberty or the means to organize a press conference in their defence. So there's no real way of hearing or knowing the accused's side of the story.

I had instructed my family against speaking to the media. The version of the cops is held to be the gospel truth until the court verdict is delivered. No wonder so many cases that the police claim are 'watertight' in their press conferences fall flat in a court of law.

Every time I cried in front of Asha, she would console me like a mother. Often, she would get me wafers and bourbon biscuits from the jail canteen. On the days I was fasting, Asha would arrange for some bananas and milk for me. Family members were allowed to visit us once in a week, between 3.30 p.m. and 5.30 p.m. A lawyer could visit every day if required. Asha's daughter and grandson came to see her one day. But after the meeting, Asha returned to the barrack with tears in her eyes.

'What happened?' I asked her.

'My grandson wants to know when his *nani* will be back home,' she said and wept.

I tried to console her. 'Is your daughter coping well?'

'Yes. Her in-laws are very understanding. My son is in Bengaluru. He is about to get married soon. I hope the police don't arrest him.'

'Don't worry,' I said. 'Everything will be okay.'

Asha's case was registered by the Economic Offences Wing, and was being heard in the court at the Azad Maidan police station premises. The police had filed a charge sheet against her, but she hadn't secured bail yet. On a day of a court visit, Asha was under considerable stress.

'The complainants take out a *morcha* against me during every visit,' she said. 'They shout slogans.'

I tried to pep her up. 'But you will also meet your husband. And your daughter will get home-cooked food for you.'

'I am scared,' she said.

'What worse can happen to us?' I said. 'We are in hell already.'

That somewhat soothed her, and she went to court in better spirits. When she returned that day, she told me that a lot of people had turned up against her and shouted slogans for the judge to hear.

'Oh, forget it, Asha Aunty,' I said. 'What did your family say?'

She replied that her husband had joked about her greying hair, and they had shared a good meal.

'Tell Ramesh Uncle that once we are free,' I said, 'I will come over to eat his specially cooked veg biryani.'

'We will also make some *kopra pak* for dessert.' Asha smiled. 'Just for you.'

*

Jaya Chheda tried her best to break the bond between Asha and me. Jaya was always waiting for me to make a mistake, so that she could screw me over. But I spent most of my time praying, and stayed away from all trouble.

'Do the two of you gossip about me?' Jaya would ask Asha.

'No,' Asha said. 'We only chant the name of Bajrangbali.'

Soni Ajwani would often join Asha and me in the veranda. She was roughly my age, had coloured blonde hair, and when I first saw her, she was wearing a white shirt and jeans. She was also lodged in Barrack No. 5. Soni had lived as a paying guest in a bungalow at Pali Hill. She was arrested by the Economic Offences Wing for duping businessmen by selling them fake airline tickets. Her aged father could not run around for her bail. Her sister lived in Dubai, and when she would come to Mumbai, she would do the legwork for Soni's release. She was also the accused in cases wherein cheques had bounced. I never saw Soni crying or emotionally vulnerable. She would often talk about her favourite restaurants like Mini Punjab and Barbecue Nation.

'Do you go pubbing?' she asked me once.

'No,' I said. 'I don't drink anyway.'

Her PG was right next to Karisma Kapoor's apartment. Inmates would often ask her about the film stars in Bandra. Soni never spoke a lot, but I derived a lot of emotional support from her. She was one of the few educated people in the jail, and the only one with whom I could hold a sensible conversation.

*

Asha and I believed the barren tree in the compound to be a form of Hanumanji. When the tree would be filled with leaves and flowers again, we believed, we would be set free. This thought gave us a sense of security, and the faith that God would smile upon us some day and give us back our freedom. Months passed. And eventually, leaves started appearing on the branches. I recognized then that it was a neem tree. Small yellow flowers blossomed upon it slowly.

22

MY WORLD WAR III

Our legal strategy was to file for bail after the police filed the charge sheet. Jayesh had an inkling that the sessions court would reject my plea. He believed we had a better chance in the high court. The charge sheet was filed towards the end of February 2012. With clouds of uncertainty hovering like demons, I collaborated with Jayesh to prepare our rebuttal to the allegations on the charge sheet. But even as we stepped into March, Jayesh did not apply for bail. FSL reports of my laptop and phone were pending. We did not know what those reports would throw at us. Every passing day was filled with frustration.

Jayesh and I agreed on hiring the services of Senior Advocate Sudeep Pasbola. Drafting a bail application at his office implied a significant legal expense. The arguments would be charged separately. I conveyed to my family to hand over the requisite funds to Jayesh. Pasbola's office began drafting the application. But even by April 2012, my bail application had not seen the corridors of the sessions court. Raja Thakur, who was a member of my legal team, came to meet me for a mulaqaat on one Saturday.

'Go ahead and file my bail application,' I said.

He looked at me as if I had committed sacrilege. 'Jayesh won't be too happy if we bypass him.'

'Where the fuck is he then?'

'He is visiting Ganpatipule for his daughter's first birthday.'

'I can't rot in here for ever!' I said. 'Get the application moving!'

Raja sensed my seriousness and filed the bail application on the next Monday, 7 April 2012. Predictably, Jayesh returned from his holiday and threw a tantrum during our next meeting.

'What was the urgency?' Jayesh asked. 'You could have waited.'

'For how long?'

'It is not as if you'll get bail tomorrow.'

'Exactly. What if the sessions court rejects? Who knows how long the high court process will take? We need to move faster.'

'The FSL reports are pending,' he said.

'The FSL reports can go to hell,' I said. 'I am tired of waiting. Get the argument dates from Pasbola sir.'

After a big fight in which I hurled a number of expletives at Jayesh, he finally saw my point and agreed to move ahead with the bail plea. But he came to meet me again after a couple of days to discuss an important development. He wanted to engage the services of Advocate Niranjan Mundargi for the bail instead of Sudeep Pasbola.

'Why?' I asked.

'The FSL reports have arrived. There are no incriminating findings against you. I have discussed the case with Mundargi already. He says we have a fair chance of success in the sessions court itself.'

I was aware that Niranjan Mundargi was a high court counsel. His fee would be much higher. But I knew I could trust Jayesh with my life. He had a free hand in making these decisions. After all, he was more of a friend than my lawyer. He would never misguide me.

'Get the dates for the argument, then,' I said.

Jayesh smiled. 'We'll start around the end of May.'

*

One day, I was chatting with Asha Pardeshi in Byculla Jail when Seema Kapoor approached me. She had been arrested for heading a prostitution racket. She had already secured bail and was about to be released in a few days.

'Here's my number,' she told me. 'Call me when you are out.'

'Why?' I asked.

She ran a finger down my cheek. 'A beautiful girl like you, my dear, should make at least a lakh every week.'

Even though I thought I had seen everything during all these months inside this facility, Byculla Jail never failed to surprise me. However, Seema's words did not shock me because I had been through worse humiliation during this ordeal. I merely stared at Seema, my heart beating fast in anger at her proposition.

'You'll serve only high-profile clientele,' she said. 'Politicians. Actors.'

I took a deep breath as I heard the 'perks' of her job offer. I wanted her to leave. She got the signal and walked away. Asha Pardeshi was looking away out of embarrassment. As soon as Seema left, a tear rolled down my cheek. People were offering me prostitution jobs now! Is that what my life had become?

Later that night, sounds of marriage processions and the tempting scents from roadside eateries wafted into Barrack No. 2. There were three windows with iron rods in the barrack, high up the walls and beyond the reach of the inmates. As I had often done on other nights, I thought of the world outside and made up my mind to never venture anywhere close to Byculla once I was out of this living hell.

*

To cover the ever-growing legal expenses, my family decided to sell off my grandmother's ancestral silver jewellery and heirlooms that had been in the family for at least a century. My grandfather had borne most of the costs of my case. A 'court group' had been created within my family and included those who were supporting me through the trial. The group would have lunch at Chetna Hotel after my hearings. We had all managed to grow closer during this tribulation. My grandfather would cover travelling expenses for some of my relatives in the court group as they were not from a financially sound background. The house was also running on my grandfather's investments. But there was the definite crunch of hard cash. My fixed deposits and savings had already been used. Yet, I protested against selling the silver. My aunt convinced me that it was necessary. Much to my guilt, the silver was sold for a sum of Rs 5 lakh.

As Jayesh had promised, the arguments for my bail began towards the end of May 2012. The hearings would be held once in four to five days. Niranjan Mundargi played a crucial role in refuting the allegations of the prosecution. He submitted that the SMS that I had allegedly sent to J. Dey was not on record. No complaint had been lodged by the deceased or on his behalf with respect to that SMS. There was a huge gap in the date on which the SMS was sent and the day of the murder.

Mundargi then came to the confession of a witness who had stated that I had instigated Chhota Rajan for the murder of J. Dey. He contested that the incriminating portions were concocted by the police and were not a part of the transcript of the intercepted communication that had been placed on record.

As for the statement of another witness about my role in assisting Chhota Rajan with the crime, Mundargi argued that the statement showed communication between the witness and Chhota Rajan on two occasions after a gap of one or two days. He submitted that the incriminating portion about my role did not find a place in the first communication, and appeared to have been concocted in the second.

The information that I had allegedly supplied to Chhota Rajan was freely available on the Internet. Another accused, Vinod Asrani, alias Vinod Chembur, had already identified J. Dey to his shooters by hugging J. Dey at a bar, days prior to the assault.

The prosecution had alleged that I had repeatedly tried to contact Chhota Rajan through Paulson, another accused in this case. Mundargi contested that there was no need for me to establish such contact, and even if it was presumed that I tried to establish contact, it could be for my professional work as a crime reporter.

He also brought up the two calls that I had received from the number +3444 on 25 May 2011. These were the incoming calls through which I had conducted an interview with Chhota Rajan in my professional capacity and in the presence of my editor, Hussain Zaidi. This interview was printed in the *Asian Age* on 26 May 2011 under the headline 'Rival Don Calls, Says Dawood Left Pak 5 Years Ago'.

The prosecution took their own time to file a reply. Public Prosecutor Raja Thakare submitted that I had transgressed my limits as a reporter, and I had added fuel to the fire. The statement of the witnesses was sufficient material to establish my role in the case. The absence of incriminating portions would be explained by the witnesses during the trial. He submitted that the boarding pass of my vacation to Sikkim had not been filed. He also contested that it was not necessary for every conspirator to know the role of other conspirators. To illustrate, he used the analogy of a city bus in which any passenger may board and get down at any time. Near the end of June, the defence and prosecution had both played their hands. It was up to Judge S.M. Modak to decide if I deserved bail or jail.

On 27 July 2012, the neem tree was blooming with life. Happiness coursed through me when I glanced at that tree. Most of my family turned up in court for a decision on the bail plea. Thankfully, the media was not allowed inside. I came out of the court with tears in my eyes. A court reporter from a national daily walked up to me.

'Your bail must have been rejected, right?' she asked.

The question stabbed me like a knife in my gut. She seemed dejected to hear from my uncle that my bail plea had been accepted! The next day, the media was full of reports that the prime accused in the J. Dey murder case had been granted bail. The media never reported that I got bail because there was no incriminating evidence against me. They had forever floated the theory that I was primarily seeking bail on medical grounds for being asthmatic and for being a single mother.

The next day, the media turned up in full force outside Byculla Jail in the hope of getting a picture of me walking out. A constable told me that a media van was positioned outside. Extra police bandobast had been made. But Jayesh had already told my family that bail did not mean I would walk out the next day as I had to give a surety of Rs 1 lakh, and the procedure would take some time. The media seemed to have missed this detail. My anxiety increased manifold during this period. I kept imagining that the police would come up with some fake evidence or new angle to save face. In the meantime, to my surprise, Dr Khan, the jail doctor, had me admitted to the J.J. Hospital, but they put me into the TB ward, with patients coughing all around. Later, I came to know that inmates are generally admitted in this ward first, and later, depending upon their disease, are shifted to different wards.

Just like a patient admitted in hospital wants to go home at the earliest, I wanted to return to the world I had got used to over the past ten months. I kept pleading with the hospital authorities to send me back to jail. Two trainee doctors wanted to check on me, but I was so suspicious that I never allowed them to touch me. I did not sleep a wink for two nights. I was glad that the media wasn't aware that I had been admitted to J.J. Hospital, else they would set up camps outside it. On the third day, I was sent back to Byculla Jail.

On 9 August 2012, I took permission from the court to speak to my son who was in his hostel in Panchgani. I told him that I would walk out of jail in a day or two.

On 11 August, around 7.00 a.m., the jailer Pushpa Kadam called me to her cabin. I suspected that she was calling me because I had volunteered to cook *sabudana khichdi* that was to be served in jail.

She gave me a wry smile. 'Your packet has arrived.'

'What packet, madam?'

'The memo for your release on bail,' she said. 'Get your packing done by 10.00 a.m.'

I could have danced my way back to the barracks, but I had grown so superstitious that I didn't want anyone to know. I took a bath and dressed in the new suit that my aunt had brought for this occasion. Paromita noticed the spring in my step. 'Your memo arrived?' she asked. I nodded. She hugged me.

Around 10.00 a.m., one of the inmates, Pinki, arrived with a chit of names of those who were going to be released that day. She shouted loud enough for all the inmates to hear. 'Jigna Vora *sutli!*' (Jigna Vora released).

Those words were music to my ears. Paromita asked Pinki to let all the barracks on all the floors know about this news. The Africans formed a circle and danced to celebrate my release. Some of the inmates wanted to keep my belongings for good luck. They took over my unused packets of toothpaste, soap and even the unused sanitary pads! I hugged everyone and walked out of the barracks. In the judicial area, I ran into Ajay Sawant, who was an officer from the Crime Branch. The mere sight of him made me shiver. Was he here to cancel my bail?

'I am here for Abu Jindal,' he said. 'Don't be scared. Your relatives are waiting outside.' Abu Jindal was an accused in the 26/11 Mumbai Attacks.

I heaved a sigh of relief. When I finally walked out, I turned around to look at the tall iron gates. I swore to myself that I'd do everything possible to not enter Laal Gate again. I would never visit Byculla again! Strangely, there was not one media personnel present to watch me walk out. But my entire family had turned up in two cars. We sped home as fast as we could. When I reached my building, I looked up at the window of my house and shouted for Leo. The lazy pug rushed down the stairs and began licking my face.

A day after I came home, my grandmother was taken ill. While she was resting in the living room, I noticed a steady stream of media personnel gathering below. But I chose to ignore it all and tried to catch a quick nap to ease a splitting headache. My neighbour rang the doorbell urgently. When my grandmother opened the door, the neighbour was gasping for breath. 'The police are here again,' she said.

Soon, a female ACP and the senior police inspector of Pant Nagar police station were outside my door and asking for me. I woke up from the commotion and walked out of my bedroom, trembling at the sight of the police. Were they here to arrest me again? Had my bail been cancelled so soon? What would they accuse me of this time? But the officers seemed concerned about me and asked about my health. My landline rang at that precise moment. It was Jayesh, and he sounded worried.

'Is everything okay?' he asked.

'The police are at my door again,' I said. 'What's going on?'

'Your investigating officer, Mahale, called me to check on rumours that you had committed suicide.'

'What!'

'Yes, and apparently there was also a rumour that your body had been taken to Rajawadi Hospital.'

'That explains the cops and the media.'

'I'll inform Mahale that you are safe,' he said and hung up.

I spoke to the ACP. They confirmed that such news was doing the rounds and they were only there to check. I thanked them for their concern and went back to sleep.

A national daily published a report stating that I was suffering from depression. Post-bail, I was under court orders not to talk to the media. It was the best thing to happen to me. Newspapers, magazines, television channels had blatantly announced that if convicted, I was likely to receive a death sentence. I wondered if the media would ever stop maligning me.

23

RETURN OF RAJAN

After being on the run for twenty-seven years, Rajendra Sadashiv Nikhalje, alias Chhota Rajan, was handcuffed in Bali, Indonesia's picturesque holiday island, on 25 October 2015. His arrest and the deportation that followed was covered in great detail and followed by most people in India. It was a significant development for some people, especially in India's financial capital Mumbai, where the self-proclaimed Hindu don had run havoc in the 1980s. Even after he fled the city in 1988, the don had continued to have a hold. From extortion and smuggling to drug trafficking and assault, the mobster's men ensured that his terror spread. The don had been named in the murders of more than seventeen people. One of them was J. Dey.

Born and brought up in Tilak Nagar in Chembur, Chhota Rajan started out selling tickets in black at a cinema hall in his locality. From being a petty thief,

he graduated to serious crime after joining the gang of
Rajan Nair, aka Bada Rajan. After Bada Rajan's murder,
Chhota Rajan took over the leadership and also the
moniker. Rajan became a much-dreaded name after he
started working for gangster Dawood Ibrahim. But their
association turned sour soon after the 1993 serial blasts
in Mumbai. The split was followed by the biggest gang
rivalry that the city had ever seen. From gang wars to
murders and police-led encounters caused by tip-offs
about rival gang members, the ugly bloodbath continued
for a very long time.

*

I was in a *vaastu* assignment in Navi Mumbai when I saw
a *Times of India* news alert on my phone: 'Chhota Rajan
Detained in Bali.'

The news flash distracted me completely from the task
at hand. I called Jayesh. He was completely oblivious to the
development.

'The television people show such news every day,' he
said. 'Most are rumours.'

Momentarily, Jayesh seemed to be right because there
were updated news alerts that said the man detained in
Bali could be Cyanide Mohan, the serial killer who had
murdered twenty-three women. But then the Bengaluru
Police soon rubbished the reports stating that Cyanide
Mohan was very much in their custody.

Subsequently, it was confirmed that the man who had been arrested was indeed Chhota Rajan. He was travelling under the identity of Mohan Kumar when was apprehended at the Indonesian airport after he arrived from Australia.

India's celebration of nabbing a notorious gangster felt like a stab wound in my stomach. The first and foremost thought in my mind was that the trial would now be delayed. Then I wondered what Chhota Rajan would say when he would be quizzed in the J. Dey murder case. There was no denying that whatever Chhota Rajan said would be treated as gospel truth. When he said Jigna had sent an email to him, everyone considered it true. When he said Jigna instigated him, everyone accepted it too. I was not prepared for another twist. I wanted all this to end.

*

On 6 November 2015, Chhota Rajan was brought to Delhi in an Indian Air Force Gulfstream-III aircraft. It was the first time that Chhota Rajan would be tried in any case. I was closely following the news developments. Unable to quell the storm within me, I would call Jayesh each time an uneasy, curious question crossed my mind. At times, he would calm me down and answer me, but there were also moments when he would get irritated.

The media was reporting on the Chhota Rajan case every day. There were speculations and theories around how the elusive don could have been caught so easily.

There were reports on how the Arthur Road Jail was being prepared to house him. But the Maharashtra government came up with a surprising twist. They decided to hand over all his cases to the Central Bureau of Investigation (CBI), India's premier investigating agency. Chief Minister Devendra Fadnavis had called for a high-level meeting with the top cops and it was followed by the announcement:

India is a signatory to the UN Convention against Transnational Organized Crime which mandates international co-operation on transnational organized crime, and Chhota Rajan was arrested under this convention. The CBI is the nodal agency for India under this convention, and hence the government has decided to transfer all cases in Mumbai and Maharashtra to the CBI. Once it has been decided to hand over all cases to the CBI, it is the CBI chief's decision whether to keep him in Delhi or bring him to Mumbai . . .

The Hindu had reported, adding that Mumbai Police had compiled a dossier of over seventy cases, including twenty under the MCOCA.

Chhota Rajan was eventually put into a high-security cell at the Tihar jail. The transfer of cases to CBI triggered a new round of debate by the political parties.

'Chief Minister Devendra Fadnavis had time and again said that Rajan will be brought to Maharashtra and even allotted a block in Arthur Road Jail (in Mumbai) to lodge him. It seems the CM was making all these statements and taking decisions without consulting the Centre,' a senior Congress leader was quoted in the *Indian Express*. 'This means there is a complete lack of coordination between the Centre and the state government, though BJP is in power in both places. This is most unfortunate', he added.

With news of the CBI's involvement, my brain went off on another tangent. Would the CBI now arrest me? Would they file a new charge sheet against me? Would I be sent to Byculla Jail? Or some other jail? I called Jayesh with my new set of questions.

'It is obvious that the CBI will question you. But there will be no arrest,' Jayesh told me, unhappy at having to answer more of my queries. 'We will face whatever comes our way,' he said.

I didn't have the courage to tell him that I was not prepared. What if I had to go back to prison? How could I ever be prepared to face that?

24

THE TRIAL

Life after bail was pleasant. Amidst all that I was forced to go through, I kept a positive attitude by counting my blessings. The evidence against me was weak. But the wheels of justice turn too slowly in our country. I had no clue when my innocence would be proved, and could only find solace in the conditional bail that had been granted to me. The court had ordered me not to travel out of Mumbai. On the first and third Monday of every month, I had to visit the Unit One office at the Crime Branch and mark my presence. Failure to comply with these two conditions would lead to the cancellation of my bail. On my first visit to the Crime Branch after bail to mark my attendance, the officers were professionally polite in their dealings with me. I took that as a positive sign.

I had made many *mannat*s in jail to visit temples and other religious places once the bail was through. But I was legally confined to the jurisdiction of Mumbai, and not even allowed to go to Thane or Vashi. While in jail, I had vowed to visit a religious place called Titwala in Thane. Jayesh filed an application in court for this, and it was surprisingly approved. Another application for visiting Rajasthan was also approved, but I had to submit the itinerary, my tickets, proof of hotel bookings and contact details before I was allowed to travel. My court hearings were scheduled once in fifteen days. I would rarely take an exemption from attending a hearing.

In March 2013, I filed an application seeking discharge from the case. The lack of evidence against me was clear, and I saw no reason to face a lengthy trial. But the application was rejected by Judge A.S. Pansare. The entire procedure took time because forensic reports of my phone and laptop were pending, and the official response from Google on my email activity was also awaited. But the main criteria for rejection was that two witnesses had given statements against me, and more light could be shed on this aspect only when the trial began.

The first witness had claimed that J. Dey had shown him an SMS that I had allegedly sent and which reportedly said in Marathi: *Tu swatala shana samajhto kaay?* The person who sent it to J. Dey was asking if he thought he was too clever in a derogatory manner. The SMS had not been retrieved in the forensic analysis. Only a CDR entry had shown up for an SMS I had sent to J. Dey in April 2010, more than a year before J. Dey was killed. The

SMS for which the CDR was available had been sent in the presence of Hussain Zaidi, and was about a completely different topic related to a crime story.

The second witness had claimed that Chhota Rajan had told him that I had sent J. Dey's bike number, photo and office address to Chhota Rajan. My lawyer argued there was no evidence to support this theory, but the judge wanted to delve deeper into the testimonies of these witnesses, which was only possible during the trial. The rejection meant that I had to face a trial, but was in no way a reflection of my guilt in the case. I discussed with Jayesh about going to the high court for appeal, but Jayesh felt it was better to face the trial rather than risk a setback in the high court. A high court application meant spending more money to engage appropriate lawyers. 'Okay,' I told Jayesh. 'Let's face the trial.'

For each court hearing, I had to stand with the ten other accused, which included the dreaded shooter Satish Kalia. It was one of the most humiliating experiences of my life to be lined up like that, and I had to go through it at every hearing. Everyone in the sessions court knew me well as a journalist. But now, they look at me pitifully or with scorn. The fifth floor of the sessions court was designated for only MCOCA cases. Hard-core criminals would swagger down the corridors without a hint of fear in their eyes, while I would shiver as I made my way to the courtroom. My manner of dressing also changed, and I would cover myself from top to bottom, and wear a dupatta to all court hearings.

In 2013, an accused in the Aurangabad arms haul case escaped from the sessions court premises. He was also being tried by Judge A.S. Pansare. After this incident, Judge Pansare moved his cases to the high-security courtroom constructed in Arthur Road Jail. It was the same jail where the 1993 bomb blasts case was heard, where I had covered all the proceedings as a journalist. My thoughts strayed to my interactions with Sanjay Dutt. I wondered what he would be thinking about me now.

During those days, my entry to these premises was always graceful and respectful. The staff at Arthur Road Jail knew me. Now, I had to bend my head down and avoid eye contact as I passed them. To top it all, my case was to be heard in the same room where Mumbai attacks terrorist Ajmal Kasab's trial was held. The courtroom had been constructed as per international standards because the case of the Mumbai terror attacks of 2008 was covered by reporters from across the globe. The fresh coat of paint and split air conditioners did not give me any comfort. My stomach hurt when I thought how a dreaded terrorist who had killed so many innocent people had sat in this very room, where I was sitting now.

Between 2013 and 2015, the date for the next hearing kept being delayed. Earlier, I would use a radio taxi to get to court, but my finances had taken a hit in the past few years. I got a second-class local train pass to travel to court and thus save money. Now my applications for travel outside the city were mostly allowed by the court. My family members planned another trip to Nepal, to visit the famous temple of Pashupatinath on the banks of the River Bagmati in Nepal. More or less, it was the same group with whom I had visited Sikkim in June 2011, when J. Dey was shot dead. But this time, the judge refused my application. He could not allow me to visit Nepal, or Dubai for that matter, since I was an accused in a case of organized crime, and the underworld had presence in such locations. I pleaded that my tickets were already booked. The judge asked why I had booked the tickets. How was I supposed to explain that my previous trips were approved only after I provided proof of my itinerary? I dropped out of the trip to Nepal, promising myself a visit to Pashupatinath later.

On 8 June 2015, charges were framed in the J. Dey murder case. All the accused were lined up and the charges were read to them. I, Accused No. 11, was asked about my stand on charges that I had instigated Chhota Rajan to murder J. Dey, and that I had supplied the underworld don with J. Dey's details that had helped him execute the crime. I firmly pleaded not guilty. That afternoon, I came back home and dwelled on what lay ahead. Now that the charges had been framed, a day-to-day trial was inevitable.

On 9 June 2015, I was sipping a cup of tea in my living room and skimming through the newspapers, which were full of reports that charges had been framed against Jigna Vora. I explained to my grandfather how the case would now proceed. He was a source of eternal strength for me. Around 10.30 a.m., my mother called on my cellphone from the landline in her room. Her health had deteriorated over the past few months. Her diabetes had worsened. She would constantly cough, and the doctors suspected it was tuberculosis. We had conducted some medical tests, but the reports were still awaited. In a month, her weight had dropped from 100 kg to 50 kg. The weakness had made her bedridden, and she needed a bedpan on most days.

When I went into her room, she appeared to be in great distress. She asked me to take her to the toilet. I led her inside, seated her and stood outside the ajar door. Even from inside the toilet, she was calling out my name continuously. I had constantly been taking care of her needs through her ailments. My grandfather could obviously not help her with going to the washroom, changing her clothes, or bathing her. So, I had stepped in. But on that day, as she kept calling me continuously while inside the toilet, I lost a bit of my patience and replied to her in an irritated tone. I craved for a breather from the constant pressure of caretaking. Anyone who has ever taken care of an old, ailing person will understand how stressful it can get. I had my own demons to fight: a murder charge, a lost career, no bank balance and dwindling savings. All of this may not justify my snapping at her, but I was fighting hard to keep my sanity through what I was dealing with.

A deep breath calmed me down. I helped my mother out of the toilet and put her back to bed. Then I went back to the living room. The tea had gone cold. So, I made some more tea and served a cup to my mother too, who thanked me for the warm drink. She also read the newspaper. Around noon, she called me again. Every bone in her fragile body was now trembling. She complained of severe chest pain.

She coughed loudly and struggled to catch her breath. 'Take me to hospital.'

For so long, I had been trying to convince her to get admitted to a hospital. She had stubbornly refused. She was adamant on paying her own medical expenses, which I had explained to her was not possible as she had spent most of her life as a housewife. Her counter to that explanation was to sell all her jewellery to pay her hospital bills. Earlier, when I had had a serious conversation about this, she had flatly refused any treatment in a hospital. She had probably lost the will to live over the last few months. She was depressed and would pop nearly fifty pills a day for her various ailments. But now was not the moment for this argument. She was in tremendous pain.

I began to rub her chest and called up our family doctor. He arrived in fifteen minutes and examined my mother. He made no serious observation, but gave her an injection and asked me to take her to the hospital. I looked at my mother. Her eyes were wide open with the realization of how much her condition had worsened. I called up a friend to help me. Then, I called an ambulance, which arrived in about thirty minutes. The paramedics pulled my mother on to a stretcher and led us down the building. My mother was awake and spoke to me as we climbed down the stairs.

'Will I survive?'

'You'll be fine, Maa,' I said. 'We'll get your medical check-ups done. You'll be back home in three days.'

I sat in the back of the ambulance with my mom. My friend sat in front with the driver. Ashirwad Heart Hospital was hardly five minutes away from my home. As I entered the hospital, I looked back and saw my mother being carried on the stretcher. She was looking right at me. Eyes open wide, lips pursed crookedly. Something was terribly wrong. 'Maa . . .' I said softly and cried. A doctor rushed over, and my mother was taken to the emergency room. Around 1.20 p.m., they tried to resuscitate her and put her on a ventilator. By 1.45 p.m., I had returned home to tell my grandfather that my mother was no more. By 2.30 p.m., her body was back home. Her death had happened in a matter of hours. It was all too quick. I arranged for her final rites and stayed at home for fifteen days. To this day, I choke to tears thinking that I spoke harshly to my mother on the last day of her life.

*

I hardly got any time to mourn. The case was on and I had to throw myself into it. A few witnesses had deposed, but Public Prosecutor Raja Thakare excused himself, citing excess workload and other reasons. This delayed the trial. Chhota Rajan's deportation and the transfer of cases to the CBI also led to more delays in my trial. In February

2016, the CBI filed a charge sheet against Chhota Rajan. But they did not have a public prosecutor in place! After considerable wait, Pradeep Gharat was appointed as the public prosecutor for all Chhota Rajan's cases. But now that we had a public prosecutor, the judge was changed. Judge Sameer Adkar was appointed to hear all cases involving Chhota Rajan. The courtroom was also shifted back to the sessions court, to Room No. 57. The witnesses started deposing. The initial witnesses were those who were a part of my panchnama. After all, hadn't the media made me into a prime accused? Witnesses against Chhota Rajan began deposing. His wife, Sujata, was also called to court. But I had taken an exemption from attending the hearing on that day.

Three witnesses were crucial to my fate: Nikhil Dixit—to whom J. Dey had shown the SMS I had purportedly sent; Manoj Shivdasani—who had conversed with Chhota Rajan on phone, when my name had allegedly come up; and Aariz Chandra, to whom Chhota Rajan had allegedly said that I had emailed him J. Dey's photo, bike number and office address. All these witnesses had given such statements to the police. However, statements given before police are not admissible as evidence in court as they can be obtained under duress. What mattered now is what these witnesses would say in court, and if their versions could stand the cross-examination of the defence. After discussion with Jayesh, I approached senior lawyer Prakash Shetty to be the defence counsel for my trial. He was a methodical and calm lawyer and known to be a master in the art of cross-examination.

Nikhil Dixit appeared in court on 3 May 2017. I almost failed to recognize him because he had grown his hair and it was in a ponytail. Public Prosecutor Pradeep Gharat began the examination. Sitting at the back, I silently began chanting the *Hanuman Chalisa*. As part of his introduction, Nikhil confirmed that he had met J. Dey in 2002, and the senior reporter had been a mentor to him in crime reporting. Nikhil also admitted to knowing me as a journalist and meeting me around 2006–07.

'Is Jigna Vora present in court today?' Gharat asked. 'Can you identify her?'

Nikhil pinpointed a finger towards the back of the courtroom, where I was seated with the other accused. Suddenly, necks turned and the entire room was staring at me. But by now, I had grown used to such humiliation. Then, Nikhil admitted that J. Dey had *shown* him the alleged SMS that I had sent. On being asked about the contents of the SMS, he replied in English, 'You think you are too smart or what?'

The PP continued his examination of the witness on other topics related to the case. Then, defence counsel Prakash Shetty began the cross-examination. He eased Nikhil into the probe of the SMS, during which Nikhil admitted that he did not know Jigna Vora's mobile number. He did not remember if Jigna Vora's number was stored in his mobile phone. No, he did not remember if any calls had been exchanged between him and Jigna Vora. He did not remember the date on which J. Dey had shown him the SMS sent by Jigna Vora. He did not verify the mobile number of the person who had sent the SMS or who had received the SMS. And no, he had not actually seen the SMS, contrary to what he had said earlier. J. Dey had only *told* him about such an SMS. Yes, in his words, it would be true to say that he was not aware of the contents of the SMS.

I heaved a huge sigh of relief. Prakash Shetty continued with the cross-examination. All along, I had wondered if Nikhil had told the police that he had seen the SMS under any kind of pressure. But again, he put it on record that it would be incorrect to say that he was deposing falsely against Jigna Vora under directions of the police or the CBI. After the hearing, I thanked Prakash Shetty profusely. He smiled and said, 'This is how the truth unfolds.'

This was a big development and a very positive one in my defence. Guess how many newspapers reported it?

Zero.

*

The prosecution had lined up another witness, Rajesh Kadam, who was from the HR and Admin of the *Asian Age* when the murder had taken place. On the day of his deposition, Rajesh was unusually cold towards me. He had brought along the attendance register, which was proof that I had gone on leave without notification to the HR, and then returned on my own. The prosecution wanted to build a case that I had deliberately gone to Sikkim on that day because I was aware that J. Dey would be killed on 11 June 2011. But under Prakash Shetty's cross-examination, Rajesh admitted that the general norm in the office was that reporters were supposed to inform their direct supervisors when proceeding on leave, and a separate notification to HR/Admin was not mandatory. And then it was presented to the court that in keeping with this norm, I had informed the resident editor, Hussain Zaidi, about my leave, in advance and in writing over an email. Prakash Shetty kept the window open to confirm this fact with Hussain Zaidi if he were to be called as a witness for the defence. Rajesh's testimony did not damage my case at all.

Other witnesses deposed before Manoj Shivdasani was called to the stand on 23 May 2017. Quite a few reporters had turned up for his testimony because his conversation with Chhota Rajan, which had been recorded by the police, was to be played in court. Also, Manoj's statement was taken before a magistrate under Section 164 of Cr.PC, which makes it admissible as evidence in court. He was liable for perjury if he backtracked on his statement. Under examination by the public prosecutor, Manoj admitted that he was friends with Vinod Asrani, aka Vinod Chembur, who was also an accused in the J. Dey murder case but had died in 2015.

'Can you recognize your statement which was recorded under Section 164 of Cr.PC if it was shown to you?' the PP asked.

'I can say that only if the statement is shown to me,' Manoj said.

The statement, which was kept in an open envelope, was now shown to the witness. He admitted that it bore his signature on the last page. But then he went on to say that the statement was recorded in Marathi, and he did not know Marathi. When recorded, the statement was not read out to him in Hindi, a language he understood, and he had simply signed the statement. So now, the statement which was recorded in Marathi was read over and interpreted to him in Hindi.

'I do not remember the contents of the statement,' he said. 'At the time of recording of my statement, I had stated the truth.'

When the recording of his call with Chhota Rajan was played in court, the part about me emailing J. Dey's information to Rajan was not a part of it. The prosecution never made an application to try Shivdasani for perjury despite the fact that he did not remember his own statement. However, another battle had been won.

Aariz Chandra was the 100th witness in the case. He appeared only after multiple summons, as he had shifted to Delhi. My acquittal was now dependent on his deposition. He admitted that Chhota Rajan had called around August or September 2011 from the number +3444. Chhota Rajan had confessed to killing J. Dey because he suspected J. Dey was working for Dawood Ibrahim. But then, Aariz deposed that Chhota Rajan had mentioned that he (Rajan) had emailed J. Dey's photo, bike number, and two articles by J. Dey about Chhota Rajan for a popular tabloid to Jigna Vora! The judge himself was flabbergasted to hear this and asked Aariz if he needed a glass of water.

'No,' Aariz said. 'I am fine.'

The prosecution asked Aariz to repeat himself, which he did, and stated that Chhota Rajan had mentioned that he (Rajan) had emailed J. Dey's photo, bike number, and two articles by J. Dey about Rajan for a popular tabloid to Jigna Vora. In a tactical move, Prakash Shetty declined to cross-examine the witness. He wanted to give no opportunity to Aariz to change the words he had just spoken. From rows ahead, Jayesh turned around to look at me. He had a smile on his face, and gave me a thumbs-up. The prosecution's case against me had collapsed. I was close to freedom. Very close. But nothing could be taken for granted until the judgment was announced on 2 May 2018.

25

ACCUSED NO. 11 ACQUITTED

The wait for 2 May 2018 was excruciating. The media trial had taken its toll on me. J. Dey's murder, understandably, had angered his colleagues and peers, and they had played their part in raising voices for a death sentence against me. Even as per law, death sentences are reserved for the rarest of rare cases. But the media only wanted to play to the gallery, sell a few more copies, and conduct sensational prime-time debates. I confined myself to my bedroom and seldom stepped outside.

My grandfather, grandmother and my mother had all been alive when I was arrested on 25 November 2011. By the time the judgment day had neared, all of them had gone, one after another. That left me and my son against the might of the law, government and media. Though I had put up a hell of a fight, I had also gone through bouts of depression and severe anxiety. Having attended the trial punctually for the last six-and-a-half years, I had had no chance to supervise my son's academics. He had been an excellent student, scoring more than 80 per cent in his SSC exams. But now, even he could not focus properly on his HSC exams. How could I blame him? I was sure he would pass, but he had slipped so much that getting into an engineering college would be nearly impossible for him. It was his dream to become a chemical engineer. My conviction would put his future in jeopardy.

I called Jayesh to my home and discussed the possibility of a conviction. He told me there was no way I was getting convicted. Though he was confident, nothing was set in stone. He knew this as much as I did. I told him that I would sign a few blank cheques he could use to pay for my son's education and manage my legal expenses in case we had to go to the high court. Jayesh agreed to this idea with a heavy heart. Even Prakash Shetty told me not to worry. He was confident of securing a release. 'Legally, there is nothing against you,' he said. 'But in the end, you will face what is in your destiny.'

I couldn't bear to look at the calendar any more. A few days prior to judgment, a photographer from the *Mumbai Mirror* turned up at my door. I cited my bail order and refused to talk or allow a photograph. Before the verdict, a few close friends turned up to express solidarity. My best friend hugged me tightly. Maybe she was wondering if she would ever see me again.

*

On 1 May 2018, as I prepared to go to sleep, I wondered where I would be sleeping the next day. Would I be back on the hard floor of Byculla Jail, jostling for space with some of Mumbai's most hardened criminals? I had met so many new faces in jail, and all of them came rushing back to my head—Paromita, Sadhvi Pragya, Usha Maa, the dreaded Jaya Chheda, the cheerful Fatima, and the lady constables. How many of them would still be there?

The media had turned up in full force when I had been arrested. Now that Chhota Rajan was back and facing his first judgment in India, the media would virtually occupy every inch of space in the sessions court. And what if the judge really sentenced me to death? I closed my eyes and imagined a black hood being put over my face, a noose tightening around my neck, hanging by the thick rope and kicking my legs until . . . I touched my face with my hands, reassuring myself that I was still alive. Though I wished for this night to never pass, I was also tired of the anxiety. I went to sleep with the conviction that I would face my destiny, whatever it was.

The next morning, three of my friends turned up to take care of my son. I gave them strict instructions to not let him out of sight until I (or my family members) returned in the evening. I left from Ghatkopar at 9.30 a.m. with another friend. A photographer from *Mid-Day* was standing below the building. I requested him to respect my privacy at this hour and covered my face with a pink dupatta.

First, I went to Chembur to my uncle and aunt's place. There, I took the blessings of my grandfather's younger brother and his wife. My aunt applied a tika on my forehead and prayed for my release. My uncle and aunt drove along with us from Chembur to Kala Ghoda, and I did not utter a word during the entire journey. I rolled down the windows and felt the breeze blow across my face. I felt the warmth of the sun. I breathed deeply, not knowing if this freedom would last beyond the next few hours.

As the car approached the court premises, I kept an eye out for media personnel. Luckily, no journalists were hounding the entry point of the first gate. I asked my uncle to stop near Irani Hotel and made my way inside the court. But the security guards did not allow my family members through this gate and asked them to enter from the other gates.

At 10 a.m., the court was empty except for the heavy security deployment. Policemen in civil clothes began entering the premises to review the security arrangements. This was a case involving Chhota Rajan and his dreaded shooters. The dog squad had sanitized the entire fifth floor. I passed by the staircase where my grandfather had once sat when he'd come to meet me at my first hearing. I could feel his presence trying to tell me that everything would be okay, just like he would console me when he was alive.

I was sitting on the bench on the fifth floor and crying, when Jane Borges, a reporter from *Mid-Day* who was also my friend, came along and sat next to me.

She spoke a few words for moral support. I handed my phone to her as I wouldn't be allowed to carry it inside. My family members turned up too. Some relatives had travelled from far away. But they were not allowed into the courtroom. Around 10.45 a.m., I trudged into the courtroom and took a seat at my regular place. The lawyers had now started streaming in.

Around 11 a.m., the judge walked in. He jocularly quipped in Marathi that he had been reading the interviews that some lawyers associated with the case were giving to the media. Even by 11.30 a.m., the media was not allowed in the courtroom. But there was a sea of lawyers inside. The other accused who were in custody had not arrived yet. Paulson was next to me, wearing a white shirt and black pant. The tension had made him loud and excited.

'What do you think will happen to us?' he said.

I ignored him at first, but he repeated himself. 'I don't know,' I said and rolled my eyes. He was only making me more nervous.

The judge asked a clerk why the *aaropi*s were not in court yet. The clerk rushed to check, and came back with a response that the accused were on their way from jail in the police vehicles. Chhota Rajan had joined via videoconferencing and he was provided with the same update, which he acknowledged. I cast a glance at Chhota Rajan's face, and the apprehension on his face was palpable. Paulson did not stop blabbering, no matter how many times I asked him to. The clock kept ticking away. My aunt had told me that *rahu kaal* would begin at 12.10 p.m. and that was worrying me now.

At 11.45 a.m., one accused entered. The others followed behind him. The judge did not even allow any time for the accused to sit. They were lined up according to their designated numbers. I was Accused No. 11, and Paulson was Accused No. 10. At least five policemen in plain clothes were guarding each accused. Jayesh looked back at me. I felt the confidence on his face had faded, or maybe he was just as nervous as I was. The judge had a small note in his hands. He started by pronouncing without wasting another minute. He said that the prosecution had proved the conspiracy.

'What is he saying?' Paulson asked me.

I felt like punching his face, but settled for saying, 'I don't know!'

Accused No. 1 was pronounced as convicted.

Accused No. 2: Convicted.

No. 3: Convicted.

Four: Convicted.

This wasn't looking good. The series of convictions continued until Accused No. 8, Vinod Asrani, was 'appended'. Vinod had died before the trial could conclude.

Chhota Rajan, Accused No. 12, was also convicted. The judgment had taken less than two minutes, an almost anticlimactic culmination of the last six-and-a-half years. My life as it had been flashed before my eyes. Was I going to walk through the Laal Gate again? My heart nearly stopped beating.

Jo Sat Baar Paath Kar Koi, Chhutahi Bandi Maha Sukh Hoi.

'Accused number 10 and 11 are acquitted,' the judge said.

What? What did I just hear?

Paulson started jumping and shouting in his *tapori* lingo. *'Apun dono acquit ho gaye na? Haan? Haan?'*

I didn't even know what to tell him. At that moment, someone from the media shouted, 'Jigna Vora is acquitted,' and rushed out to break the news to their peers. I began crying. The courtroom began to blur before my eyes.

The judge continued that no evidence had been found against Accused No. 10 and 11. My innocence had finally been proved. I was no longer an accused murderer.

I asked Jane Borges from *Mid-day* to tell my family that I was free again. Jayesh was crying. We had started our careers on the same day. My first day as a reporter in the sessions court had also been Jayesh's first day as a lawyer. Prakash Shetty's eyes were also moist. 'Happy, na?' he asked me. Truly, he was a man of few words.

I was required to post a bail bond. Once an accused is acquitted, the person is required to sign a bond saying that he/she will remain present whenever court calls upon them in the future. On Jayesh's suggestion, I went out to ask my relatives to leave, as the procedure would take until evening. The judge would first pronounce sentences for all the convicts after lunch. As I was walking out of court, the security stopped me. 'At least let me go *now*!' I said.

A constable then made way for me. All my relatives hugged me. They were all crying. Using Jayesh's phone, I called home and spoke to my son. He couldn't stop crying. But I was delighted to hear his voice, to know that I would be around him for the foreseeable future at least. My relatives left soon for their respective homes. I drank a glass of water and went back to the courtroom. Only the friend who had accompanied me through the morning stayed back. Around 5.30 p.m., I exited from the back door with my face covered in the dupatta again. I refused to talk to the media. I heard a female reporter snigger, 'She is still so arrogant.' I ignored those words, got into Jayesh's car and rolled up the black-tinted windows. Six photographers on bikes chased us till CST. I did not utter a single word throughout the journey. As the car sped along, I imagined shedding my past, bit by bit. Perhaps, somewhere during the journey, I had also lost the Jigna I knew.

Jayesh dropped me to Chembur, at my uncle's place, as we suspected that the media would have camped near my house in Ghatkopar. I took a quick nap, and it was sound sleep for the first time in six-and-a-half years. At midnight, I came back home—to my son and my freedom.

EPILOGUE

The Mystery

The first charge sheet in the J. Dey murder case was filed in December 2011. According to this 3,000-page document, Chhota Rajan was irked by two scathing articles that J. Dey had written about him, and more so about the remarks that he was an ageing don. These articles were published on 29 May 2011 and 4 June 2011.

After Dey was shot dead on 11 June 2011, Chhota Rajan called up some crime reporters and news channels. He claimed that Dey had to be killed because he had turned a traitor by joining hands with Dawood. Rajan also spoke about Dey inviting him for a meeting in London. Dey's visit to London was said to be a personal one and not a trip sanctioned by office. Rajan's trusted sources in Dubai had warned him that a death trap had been laid for him, and Rajan had cancelled the meeting on the basis of his suspicion. He also claimed that Dey had invited him for a meeting in the Philippines. But this time, Rajan's suspicion ticked him off and he made up his mind to eliminate this alleged threat to his life.

In all these theories, one thing continued to intrigue me. Satish Kalia, the sharpshooter who pulled the trigger on J. Dey, and his associates had procured the weapon from Deepak Sisodia in Nainital between 12 May and 15 May 2011. How could the articles written by Dey, which were published on 29 May 2011 and 4 June 2011, then have provoked Chhota Rajan to kill him? The only possible theory would be that Rajan had known about the Dey articles way in advance.

My only communication with Chhota Rajan was on 24 May 2011 for an official interview for a story that was published the next day in the *Asian Age*, where I worked then. This was much later than the weapon to kill J. Dey had been procured. I wondered, and I still do, about how and why my name appeared in this heinous plot at all. How had I instigated Chhota Rajan? And when exactly did I do that? I have never found an answer to this, nor did the investigators.

In 2016, the CBI filed a second charge sheet in the J. Dey murder case. Strangely, this charge sheet had no mention of the two articles that the Mumbai Police claimed had been the motive for the murder. CBI's theory claimed that Chhota Rajan plotted the murder because

Dey was writing a book on the underworld titled *Chindi: Rags to Riches*. The term *chindi* in the slang of Mumbai is a derogatory reference to something or someone of little consequence. The book apparently referred to the small beginnings of Chhota Rajan, when he had started selling movie tickets in black near Sahakar Cinema in Chembur. Reportedly, Chhota Rajan was seething at the way he was going to be portrayed in the book. Email exchanges between J. Dey and his book editor were made part of the CBI charge sheet. But J. Dey was a very private person. He was never outspoken, and pretty much kept his work and personal life a secret from anyone who did not need to know. How did Chhota Rajan then come to know about Dey's book? There hasn't been a satisfactory answer to this question.

Against me, the CBI relied on the statement of Aariz Chandra. In the judgment, the judge considered all theories and generally agreed to Chhota Rajan's version of events. Chhota Rajan's interviews played a key role as an extrajudicial confession. In recent times, the Supreme Court of India has ruled that an extrajudicial confession is a 'weak piece of evidence', but can be acted upon to convict a person if a court is satisfied that it is voluntary.

The judge observed that in no interview had Chhota Rajan claimed that I, Jigna Vora, Accused No. 11, had instigated him to murder J. Dey. In an interview to NDTV, Chhota Rajan had made no mention of my name. About ten days before my arrest, when Chhota Rajan spoke to Jitendra

Dikshit, who was with Star News then, he did not mention me. When Chhota Rajan spoke to journalist Nikhil Dixit, who was Dey's best friend, he kind of lamented about making a mistake by killing Dey, but I was not mentioned in the conversation. When Dey's wife deposed in court, she spoke about some friction between her husband and an ACP of the Mumbai Police, but she did not talk about any history that existed between J. Dey and me. There was no proof of any email exchanges between Chhota Rajan and me. The mobile phones recovered from me did not have any incriminating evidence even after extensive forensic analysis. My name had only popped up in Aariz Chandra's statement to the police.

I had written a story about Dey's meeting with Dawood aide Iqbal Mirchi in London. The lead for this story had been provided by my sources in the Mumbai Police, who later claimed that I had tried to mislead their investigation by the article. The court, however, did not agree to this particular argument of the Mumbai Police.

The men who killed J. Dey were convicted. These included Satish Kalia, the dreaded sharpshooter, Anil Waghmode, who was riding the bike on that rainy day, Abhijit Shinde, Arun Dake, Sachin Gaikwad, Nilesh Shendge, Mangesh Agawane, and Deepak Sisodia, who supplied the gun. Vinod Chembur, who had allegedly identified the target to the shooters, was appended from the trial on account of his death. Chhota Rajan himself was convicted, and his interviews after the murder played a part in his conviction. Paulson Joseph, who was accused of providing SIM cards to the shooters, was acquitted. A certain Ravi Rateshwar, who was named a witness in the charge sheet filed by the Mumbai Police, was listed as an accused in the CBI charge sheet.

Rateshwar is currently based in Dubai and efforts are on to extradite him to India. Apparently, he is a close aide of Chhota Rajan. Another associate of Deepak Sisodia, Nancy Bisht, is still at large. Ravi Rateshwar and Nancy Bisht are the two wanted accused in this case till date.

The judgment spans over 600 pages. Three small paragraphs in those 600 are about me. 'There is nothing in their evidence to suggest that the Accused No. 11 had instigated the Accused No. 12 (Rajan) to commit the murder of J. Dey or that she had any other role in this offence,' the judgment stated.

Those three paragraphs restored the dignity that had been ripped away bit by bit, every day, for seven long years.

Will life be the same again? I can't tell. Can I go back to being the star reporter that I was? No. All this for a weak, malicious allegation that could not be proven. As I look back at the case, I still wonder why J. Dey was really murdered. Perhaps that will for ever remain a mystery.

ACKNOWLEDGEMENTS

First and foremost, I must thank my family members—my maternal uncle Ketan Sanghavi, maternal aunt Priti Sanghavi, Neela Bhuta, Jayesh Bhuta, and my uncle Rajesh Vora—for standing by me, rock solid during these seven years of ordeal. I really appreciate them for always being present at my court hearings while I was in custody and when I returned.

Special thanks goes to my cousin, Paresh Vora, for diligently bringing me home-cooked food for three months, prepared by Aruna bhabhi. Travelling to Byculla from Santa Cruz is never easy but he would come every day with the food. I thank all my near and dear ones who kept faith and believed in me. My grandparents, who were in their mid-eighties at that time, never questioned my innocence. I wish my mother and grandparents could have witnessed the fact that I have been proved innocent.

I am indebted to my son for not doubting me even once and grateful for understanding me in my fight for justice. It was equally tough for him to go through the humiliation.

I am thankful to Rajeev Sharma for being in my life when I was going through its worst and most difficult phase. Thanks, Rajeev, for truly loving and believing me.

I am grateful to my lawyer, Mr Prakash Shetty, for always having his ears open for me and believing in my side of the story. Thank you, sir, for giving me this second lease of life. Jayesh Vithlani for being a friend first, more than a lawyer. Thank you for patiently handling my frustration, tantrums, fears and tears right from the day of my arrest till acquittal and always being there for me.

I am grateful to my childhood friends Nilesh Vasi, Ramesh Chaudhry, Vivek Desai, and Sangeta Telekar, for always cheering me up and helping me rebuild my life. I am thankful to Rekha and Atul Parekh for supporting our family in this tough time.

I am also grateful to my police officer friends who stood beside me and prayed for me. I would also especially like to thank a police officer from Gujarat, whose absence was always present and whom my eyes would always hunt for during these seven years. I understand his dilemma but thanks for being present, albeit silently, during my struggle to prove my innocence.

Special thanks goes to Kashif Shaikh and Jyoti Shelar for putting my story into words and working so dedicatedly on this. I still remember the late-night conference calls from different corners of the city to discuss the book.

I want to thank Hussain Zaidi, my mentor, and my boss at that time, for believing in me and having my back all these years. This book couldn't have been possible without him. Thank you, sir.

Lastly, sorry to everyone, particularly my family, who had to go through all the humiliation.